# WRITE A
# NOVEL IN
# TEN MINUTES
# A DAY

Katharine Grubb

# Write a Novel in Ten Minutes a Day

Katharine Grubb

Also available
in ebook

For Billie Jauss and Brian Duxbury,
with much love

# Acknowledgements

This book would not have been written without the enthusiastic support of my family: Marc, Ariel, Miranda, Corbin, Perrin and Veronica. Thank you for making your own lunches, doing your own laundry and for not knocking on my door. But then after that, you cheered me on and celebrated with me. I love you so much!

I am also grateful for the team at John Murray Learning and MacGregor Literary for their faith in me and the occasional hand holding.

Many thanks to my critique partner, Jane Steen, for her faithful support and encouragement. I'm sure the inventor of Facebook's DMs didn't know they would be used as virtual shoulders to cry on. Thank you also to Barbara Szyszkiewicz for her helpful editing. I am so grateful for you!

And a very special thank you to Marla Cilley, the Flylady, whose passion and enthusiasm for working in ten-minute increments completely changed my life.

Also, my heart is full when I think of the wonderful experience it was to coach Brian Duxbury and Billie Jauss in the winter and spring of 2014. Our weekly emails pushed me, their confidence in me strengthened me and their affection sustained me. I'm proud of you. Congratulations on the completion of your novels!

I want to thank the passionate and joyful writers who have honoured me with their participation in the Facebook group I created: 10-Minute Novelists. In my wildest dreams, I could never have predicted how much fun hundreds of strangers could have together. I hope all of you write bestsellers and make millions. Leading you has been the single most satisfying thing I've ever done, including writing books. You are my #AuthorHappiness. (#Allthefreakingfeels!)

And to all of the hopeful novelists who want to find time to pursue their dreams: I salute you. I know you can do it.

# Contents

## Part Four: Putting it all together

# Introduction

## Octavia E. Butler

*'I just knew there were stories I wanted to tell.'*

It's easy to be intimidated by well-written novels. Let's think about our favourites, the ones that hooked us from the beginning, the ones that engaged our senses, the ones whose characters spoke in witty or fascinating dialogue. Let's think about the novels whose worlds were mesmerizing, the ones whose plot led us through twists and surprises. Let's think about the ones that compelled us to keep turning the page to lose another hour's sleep. Let's think about the novels that, when we came to the ending, made us want to weep or applaud or savour the moment a bit longer.

Could we *ever* write like that?

Perhaps, because we have a reader's perspective, we often think that the task of writing a novel ourselves is impossible. Because we think like readers, we may mistakenly believe that accomplished novelists string their words together in chronological order in one draft, with perfect sentences coming from their brains to the computer screen. Because we think this, we come to believe that our own aspirations of becoming novelists are pointless.

The reality is that writers *don't* write that way. The very best writers take each chapter, each paragraph, each line and each word and they examine it from every perspective. The very best writers look at not only what they are trying to say, but also *how* they are saying it. What readers *don't* know is that the final product is so much simpler than all the work that went into it. The book, which includes the story, the characters, the setting and the plot, was carefully *sculpted*.

Like sculptors, novelists start with big ideas. Both sculptors and novelists put much thought into their idea before they ever chip away bits of marble or write a single word. Like a sculptor, the early work of a writer may be violent and loud and messy. Later changes make it become delicate, soft and subtle. A good novel is not one that is rushed through in its writing; it is rarely written in one chronological draft. Instead, it is sculpted piece by piece, bit by bit, hammered, chiselled, filed, stroked and polished. A good writer sculpts his story over time.

Aspiring novelists today often don't have time to sculpt great novels. We have busy lives. We have children to raise and jobs to attend to and household responsibilities. We have the nagging thoughts that tell us that our dreams are not worth pursuing.

I would like to suggest that you can, without any guilt or shame, sculpt a novel in very small increments of time. You can make decisions bit by bit and then use your writing time effectively. You can take each one of the exercises in this book, work at them around your schedule, and slowly see your story come to life.

This book breaks down everything required to sculpt a story through a series of ten-minute tasks and exercises. The book is divided into four main parts:

- **Part One**, *Arranging your writing around your life* (Chapters 1–3), gives practical tips on how to carve out small pockets of time and create a space for your writing.
- **Part Two**, *Thinking like a writer* (Chapters 4–5), describes how to practise observation and description. This section explains the necessity for creating a unique voice, shows you how to implement free writing into your writing time and encourages you to pay attention to the world around you.
- **Part Three**, *Sculpting the elements of story* (Chapters 6–18), systematically explains each of the elements of story within the classical story structure and explains why mastery of these concepts is important in the creation of your story.
- **Part Four**, *Putting it all together* (Chapters 19–22), is where you will begin drafting your novel. This section allows you to apply all the principles and suggestions mentioned in the

previous chapters. It explains how to revise and edit your work and receive feedback from others. If you wish to publish, many options are discussed in this section.

At the end of the book there are lists of references and additional resources, if you need more help in your journey as a novelist.

# What is a ten-minute exercise?

Each chapter contains tasks and exercises that reinforce the concepts mentioned. Each task or exercise can be done in ten-minute increments. These exercises will help you clarify your personal vision for your novel. You will be asked to list your time commitments and think through your abilities. You will consider your organization and how you'll track your time. You'll practise observing the world around you, learn to write quickly, and tap into your unique voice. You will create the basic elements of your story and carefully consider each detail. You will learn how to draft under time constraints. You will plough through tough passages and come out victorious. You will rewrite and rewrite and rewrite again. But by the time you've finished all the exercises in this book, you will have created something beautiful.

Are ten minutes enough? Ten minutes are not enough to frighten us at the size of the task ahead. Ten minutes, instead, are enough to nurture our confidence. Ten minutes are enough time to complete one task and satisfy our creative passion. Ten minutes are a reasonable request of those who are the first to demand our time. Ten minutes won't interfere with other responsibilities. In these ten minutes, you will see the sculpting of your novel grow day by day.

But, like everything else, these ten-minute exercises require effort. They are not for the faint of heart. You will not find that every ten-minute exercise will be easy. Some will take longer, perhaps needing several ten-minute blocks. Take all the time you need. There is no rush. You have not written too few or too many words. Just answer the questions, thinking through the exercises as thoroughly as you can. Thoroughness is far more important than conciseness. This is also not a college application or a test. No one will see this but you.

In these ten minutes, you'll discover that most of what you write will be unpublishable. It's likely that you'll still be interrupted. You certainly won't make any money. And this is certainly not a book to race through in a weekend. But if you keep going, then you will see results. Your story will develop. Your plot and characters will become clearer. You will be writing a novel!

## ICONS

Here's your key to the different types of exercise and features in the book:

 **Write** exercises where you'll be asked to write something

 **Snapshot** shorter exercises or some questions to help you consider a particular aspect of your writing

 **Workshop** a series of guided questions that will help you reflect on an aspect of your writing – see below for a more detailed explanation

 **Edit** a chance to rework and strengthen a piece you've already created

 **Key quote** words of wisdom from those who know

 **Key idea** an important concept to grasp

 **Focus point** advice to take forward

 ## David Eddings, fantasy author

*'Keep working. Keep trying. Keep believing. You still might not make it, but at least you gave it your best shot. If you don't have calluses on your soul, this isn't for you. Take up knitting instead.'*

The calluses are worth it. I know that this is true because I did it myself. Around the demands of my family, I snuck in ten minutes here and there. I set timers. I stayed up late. I got up early. I worked around the responsibilities that usually come with a home-schooling mother of five and I wrote my first novel over the course of five years. The point wasn't speed; the point was that I wanted to prove to myself that I could do it.

Let's not be intimidated by the task of novel writing. Instead, focus on how you, in very small increments, can sculpt your novel bit by bit.

Throughout the book are workshop exercises that allow you to apply the principles of the chapter and create another element for your novel. This is a process of art, not science. There are no right or wrong answers. The best way to do each exercise is to set aside at least one ten-minute segment daily to work on it. No one is looking over your shoulder to see whether you are fast or slow. No one is correcting your grammar or spelling. The only measure of your success is the completion of each answer so that you can refer to it later. Sometimes it will take you longer than ten minutes to complete a workshop but the point is not to go quickly; the point is take ten minutes to finish one part of it and later another ten minutes for the next part, and so on.

You will be planning and drafting your entire novel in ten-minute increments, so it could take you a good long while to get through it, but don't let this discourage you.

Conventional wisdom says there are only two steps to writing a book: *butt in chair, hands on keyboard.* This will take time. You're creating art. This is worth doing.

The purpose of this book is to teach writers to work in very small increments. How much can be done in ten minutes? Find out! Set a timer and do this first exercise as fast as you can, working for ten minutes on each part. Don't worry about spelling, punctuation or grammar (no one is going to see this).

## Thinking about writing

1 Finish this sentence: 'I want to be a writer because …'

2 Now answer these questions: What do you think about writing in ten-minute increments? Do you think you can accomplish it? What do you think about the little bit that you've written so far?

How many words did you write? How easy was this to do? How hard was this to do? Even with this tiny bit of energy and tiny bit of time, you can accomplish something. You can do this. You can make things happen around your schedule. You can see things come together.

# PART ONE
## Arranging your writing around your life

# 1

## Envisioning and planning

Before a sculptor applies that first cut, hack or wallop to an expensive piece of marble, he's envisioned what he's doing. He has sketched. He has studied other artists. He has looked for inspiration everywhere. Unless he's a fool, he's not going to start hacking away and hope, somehow, that *David* pops out of it. So his first move has to be right.

Novelists have it much easier. We sculpt together words bit by bit to create our art. Words are far cheaper than marble, but just because they're cheap doesn't mean we shouldn't put thought and care into our choices. Like a sculptor, we should study, practise, look to other writers and create a vision before we attempt the final product.

In this chapter, you will be comparing your desire to write to a sculptor's desire to create a masterpiece.

## Toni Morrison

*'If there's a book that you want to read, but it hasn't been written yet, then you must write it.'*

## Focus point

Each of the exercises in this book should take you at least ten minutes. Self-editing or critical thoughts are not allowed. Do each exercise and answer each question as freely as possible for at least ten minutes. If you want to write for a longer time than ten minutes, then go for it!

## Envision your novel

Picture yourself at a bookstore signing. Hundreds of people are there to meet you, buy your book and get a signed copy. You're being photographed. You're getting handshakes. Some readers are potentially star-struck. What is this book about? Is it a romance? A thriller? A mystery? Is it a story that asks big questions in life? Is it a fantasy? Is it for Young Adults? Don't worry about the title, but instead take ten minutes and envision this book. What would you like the blurbs on the back to say? 'Romantic?' 'Gripping?' If you need help, start your answer like this:

*At my book signing, my book will be a _____. On the back, critics will say that it is _____. I want to be known as that writer who _____.*

## Your favourite authors

List your favourite authors, the ones to whom you'd like to be favourably compared. Why do you like them so much? Why would this comparison be important to you?

## Your favourite books

List your favourite books. Which genres are the most represented?
Would you like to write in this genre? Why or why not?

# Embracing low expectations

You may imagine that most writers must have a smoke-filled office
in which they spend their days perfecting their prose in solitude,
their only interruption the clink of the bottle on their glass as they
pour another shot of whisky, or when the cat climbs up on their
computer to walk across the keyboard, or when the post arrives
with their fan mail. This isn't the reality for most writers: many have
day jobs, families and outside obligations that drain their energy
and brainpower. Little time or energy is left for pursuing their goals.
Their interruptions are more numerous than the unmatched socks in
the endless piles of laundry.

Despite this, these writers do manage to sculpt a novel in ten-minute
increments. It might take them months or years, but they still
succeed in the end. My first novel took five years to sculpt. I wasn't
trying to get the job done quickly; I was just learning how to do it.
I was committed to giving my passion every small chunk of time I
had, so that at least I could write something. I was often discouraged
and I was often interrupted, and I probably discarded half a million
words before the finished 95,000-word book was done, but I did it.
I succeeded around homeschooling five children, baking bread and
doing laundry.

It looked like this: I set the timer on my microwave for ten minutes
and then wrote. Once the timer went off, I reset it and emptied the
dishwasher or folded a load of washing or started a meal. I also
checked on the children and made sure no one was bleeding. Once
that timer went off, I went back to the computer and got a few
sentences out. (Woe to the child who interrupted me while I wrote!)
I did this all afternoon and somehow, everything got done.

I developed this system because I wanted to do it all. I wanted to
give all to my family *and* pursue my writing dreams. I knew that if
I looked for big chunks of time or perfect conditions, they would

never come. My theory was that ten minutes were better than none at all. And if I did this six times in one day, I would have written for an hour. An hour devoted to writing seemed like a luxury.

 ## C.S. Lewis

*'If we let ourselves, we shall always be waiting for some distraction or other to end before we can really get down to our work. The only people who achieve much are those who want knowledge so badly that they seek it while the conditions are still unfavourable. Favourable conditions never come.'*

I don't believe that any writer should wait for the perfect moment, or for when the kids are older, or for huge chunks of time, or even when our offices and pets and drinking habits resemble those of famous writers. I think, instead, that setting a timer and typing like mad until it goes off is a better strategy. Doing something is better than doing nothing.

 ## Look at your typical day

Do you have a set time daily to put in at least ten minutes? Can you have more than one ten-minute session a day?

# Facing the darkness

 ## Steven Pressfield

*'If you find yourself asking yourself (and your friends), "Am I really a writer? Am I really an artist?" chances are you are. The counterfeit innovator is wildly self-confident. The real one is scared to death.'*

In his book *Do the Work* (2011), author Steven Pressfield explains that there is inside each budding author a drive to write, to create, to sculpt stories and to change the world through words. Yet, just as powerful as that drive is, there is an equally powerful drive to resist. This opposing drive can demean and diminish a writer's dream by shaking their confidence. This opposition whispers in their ear that they don't deserve this passion, they will never succeed, they shouldn't attempt writing, or that failure is their only destiny. Pressfield calls this *the resistance*.

In her book *The Artist's Way* (1992), Julia Cameron coaches budding artists to identify the source of their resistance, to substitute positive self-talk, to encourage a budding artist (or writer) to pursue their dreams without fear of judgement, condemnation, ridicule or uncertainty. She says, 'Creativity flourishes when we have a sense of safety and self-acceptance.' She describes the practical steps that artists can take to protect themselves against negativity.

Darkness and negativity are arguably the biggest blockers of success for many writers. I would like to suggest that an honest assessment of this darkness in our lives is critical to our future success.

We deserve to pursue our dreams. The desires that we have are there for a reason. Anything that opposes them may have been put there by others, perhaps those who are abusive, jealous, powerful, controlling or manipulative. This fear is a lie. If we believe it, and allow it to stifle our art, then we will be miserable. Our spirits, our souls, our destinies and certainly our future books are at stake if we do not overcome this darkness and continue to fight against it as we write.

Successful writers are overcomers. Not only have they wielded their stories, wrestled with characters, sculpted, chiselled and hammered away at their stories for months or even years, but they have also fought fears, doubts, discouragement and possible mental instability. Any published work is far more than the sum of its parts: it is also a mark of courage, of tenacity and – possibly literally – blood, sweat and tears. Each published novel could be called the trophy of a victorious battle, won despite much turmoil from within the author or from his environment.

I, too, have struggled with this. I decided, at age 38, that I would not live one more day *not* pursuing my dreams. I would not allow the negative forces behind the lies to steal one more day of victory from me. I'd rather fail miserably at writing than let my children see me *not* try out of fear. In my case, I needed to seek the advice of a therapist, read books like *The Artist's Way*, pray a lot, and disassociate myself from people around me who, as my therapist puts it, 'won't let me walk in the fullness of my awesome'. Every artist who has a shadow of negativity in their lives has to find their own way to overcome this darkness.

The following is potentially the most intimate and difficult exercise in the book, but also the most important. You may find it helpful to weaken the power of the darkness in you by explaining it to another writer, a trusted friend or a counsellor.

## Overcoming resistance

This exercise, this *facing the darkness*, is possibly one of the most challenging in the book. When you think of the darkness, that powerful resistance that is holding you back from pursuing your writing dreams, who or what is the source of it? What specific things does this darkness say to you?

For every lie others have told you, write two truths. For example, if one of the lies told to you was 'Taking time to write every day is selfish and childish', your response should be: 'It's never selfish to nurture my soul. Childish? I'm doing this so that I can return to the child-like joy I once had for my passions.'

## Your strengths and supports

This workshop will help you identify the things that will help you when you are feeling discouraged. Refer to them regularly to lift your morale.

- What are your strengths? Write down as many as you possibly can.
- Who in your life is on your side, cheering you on?
- What encouraging things have you been told about your character, your skills, your dreams and your goals?
- How do you feel about this exercise? Was it hard to face this or was it encouraging?

## Where to next?

*The next chapter will help you think about how to organize your time more efficiently so that you have time to write, fitting it in around the other demands of your life.*

# 2

## Organizing your time

Writers today rarely have the luxury of peace and quiet, solitude, and absolutely no distractions. Writers today would be foolish to wait for the perfect setting; their wait would be a long one. I think that contemporary culture and current lifestyles require writers to make the best of their situations instead – *around* the noise, interruptions and demands of family.

The exercises in this chapter are designed to help you think about how you organize your time to write. Each exercise is a chance to evaluate how you spend your days and how you can juggle obligations in such a way that you can scrape up another ten minutes for yourself here and there. Each exercise involves looking at a different part of your life. Take at least ten minutes on each one and carefully evaluate how you can organize your time more efficiently.

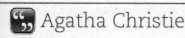
# Agatha Christie

*'The best time to plan a book is while you're doing the dishes.'*

According to tradition, the poet Samuel Taylor Coleridge awoke from a long (and probably drug-induced) sleep one night in 1797 and sat down and wrote out the first dozen lines of or so of *Kubla Khan*. Then someone came to his door and interrupted him for an hour. According to Coleridge (who put the details of this event in the introduction to the poem), his unwritten ideas were lost. Because of the interruption, he couldn't remember what he was going to write next. Poor Coleridge and poor us: those lines for *Kubla Khan* were lost for ever.

Poor Coleridge, indeed! He had quiet and solitude. He was alone, which could have been either the cause or the effect of his recreational drug use. It's hard for me to feel sorry for him (but then again, I've never written anything like *Kubla Khan* or *Rime of the Ancient Mariner*). I wonder how Coleridge would have managed the setting in which I drafted this chapter in the summer of 2013. Our home housed ten people. The day I wrote this, my family and I had an impromptu visit from an elderly aunt who said, loudly, 'Don't let me bother you!' She sat next to me and talked to my mother-in-law while I was only feet away, writing. Coleridge didn't homeschool his five children as I do. He didn't have his mother-in-law's Gospel music from the 1980s playing in the background, or someone vacuuming, or the entrance of a niece and then a nephew looking for playmates. He never wrote around discussion after discussion on whether it was a good day to go to the pool. But then again, we aren't completely sure what his drug-induced dreams were about. Maybe he did.

Another draft of this chapter was written at a noisy, crowded Starbucks in the middle of a January afternoon where everyone in Belmont, Massachusetts apparently thought coming in out of the single-digit temperature was a good idea. I had my ear buds in and my eyes on the screen, and I was doing the best I could, but this Starbucks wasn't an ideal place to write. I did it anyway. Writers in the twenty-first century have trouble, I think, feeling sorry for poor, poor Coleridge and his interruptions.

When I started writing in ten-minute increments, I conveniently had my computer in my kitchen. I was able to write for ten minutes, then attend to domestic and maternal duties for another ten, then go back to my computer. There were days when I was able to do this all day. There were days when I was able to write for only one or two ten-minute sections. There were days when I used my mindless tasks to work out the problems in my story. And there were days when I couldn't write at all.

When I was able to set my timer and write, I noticed *how fast my other work got done*. I discovered that I could load and unload the dishwasher in ten minutes. I could fold a load of laundry in ten minutes. I could plan the shopping. I could scrub potatoes. I could prepare the meat for a crockpot meal. In ten minutes I could clean a bathroom. In ten minutes I could dust two rooms. In ten minutes I could vacuum one. I discovered that the more efficient I made my other work, the more writing time I had. My life is different from Coleridge's: it's full of life and messiness and other responsibilities. Because of this difference, I have to shape my writing life differently.

## Focus point

Regardless of how great your story is or how beautifully you tell it, it will not be written unless there is time to get it done. Even if you only have time for 200 words in one ten-minute increment, that's still 1,000 words over the working week. That's 4,000 words a month. In a year, you would have 60,000 words – which is a Harlequin novel's worth, and coincidentally, the length of the book you are reading. Your dreams are worth pursuing, even in tiny chunks of time.

# Reviewing your standards

First, you have to determine your standards. How do you want your household run? If finding time to write, even ten minutes, seems like an impossible task, it may have something to do with the demands of the standards of your household. The *way* you run your household may be a killer for your creativity.

Your standard for your household is the level that you and your partner have agreed to with regard to food, cleanliness, clothing, extracurricular activities, bedtime rituals and anything else that adds to the culture of your home. Every home is different. Every home will have specific needs around these issues. Homes with small children have different needs from homes with teenagers. Single-parent homes run in a different manner from those with two parents. Some homes revolve around sports schedules. Some revolve around a child with special needs. The standard you choose is the level of necessity that your family requires. The lack of an agreed standard can often lead to misunderstandings, chaos and a possible waste of resources. All your resources are precious, but time management is the most critical when you're scraping up ten-minute increments to write a novel. Any deliberate consideration of your standards will be helpful.

For example, every family has different standards with regard to food: my family's food allergies and frugal lifestyle choices require us to cook all our meals from scratch. Every day, I need to allow for meal planning, shopping, preparation, cooking and cleaning up. A household that can eat more processed food or more takeaways will have other time and labour demands to consider.

Every time a standard is agreed to and is reinforced daily, that standard eventually, because the habit is in place, becomes the 'default' setting. Eliminating discussion saves time. The cook of the household never asks the ubiquitous 'What are we eating for dinner?' question; she always knows the answer, whether her standard is planning meals in advance or deciding to go for the microwave burritos.

You can also apply the concept of agreeing to a standard in the area of household chores. If your standard is that you can live without the rug being vacuumed, your energy towards that task can be put towards writing. If, however, you feel the need to vacuum every day, then make the time for it. Schedule it, so that this activity is in a proper place.

The purpose of standards is to see exactly where your family's priorities are, where your energy goes and how you can streamline your time.

Your standards may be so high that you have no time to do anything else. If that's the case, the your daily cleaning routine may lean toward the obsessive and you will need to let a few things go to find time to write. Or your expectation that each of your children takes soccer, ballet, karate, piano, voice *and* scouts is a ridiculously high standard – you will have *no time* to pursue your writing goals unless you are using voice-activating software that's connected to your mini-van.

On the other hand, your standards could be so low that you have no order, no plan and you just put out fire after fire. The evening meal is a constant surprise to you. You only do laundry when no one has clothes to wear. You have no place to put schoolwork or important documents or your work in progress. This is an equally destructive assault on your time.

If either extreme is a description of your home life, you may need to ask yourself questions about this. You and the other adults in your household need to agree – so that you can back each other up, set good examples and gently hold each other accountable.

This isn't a chapter on how to clean a sink or do other routine household chores. (Marla Cilley's *Sink Reflections* is the book to read on that subject.) Instead, it is a chapter on deliberate standard making – knowing who you are and how you want your home to run. Whether you write a book or not, you will still have to eat, pay bills and clean up. This chapter is about streamlining these tasks as efficiently as possible so that your time is maximized.

Not making a decision is still making a decision. If you decide not to make time to do laundry on a regular basis, then you will discover a mountain of smelly clothes (and possibly naked family members) in a matter of days. A more effective approach to laundry is to make a decision, *set a standard,* of one load a day – wash, dry, fold, put away. The small amount of time invested in doing this on a regular basis, whether it is daily, every two days or weekly (if you can get away with it) will surpass any advantage of procrastination.

# Getting your family involved

If you have children over six years old, then you potentially have assistance to help you meet your household goals. Every parent has different expectations and philosophies of child rearing. However, the task of home management is far easier with a team. It *will* take precious time to teach a child to make his bed or pick up his toys. But the time spent is an investment in the future – *your* future. A child who is taught how to be responsible at seven or eight will be able to handle bigger responsibilities at twelve and thirteen. Not only will this make your children more skilled and independent, it will raise their self-esteem and allow you to have more creative time.

If you are teaching your child an age-appropriate task, such as emptying the dishwasher, taking out the bins or dusting, there are a few key things to remember:

1 **Show them how; don't just tell them.** By allowing them to watch you perform the task, they are more likely to repeat it. Let them practise with you until they have mastered it enough to handle it without supervision.

2 **Set them up to succeed.** Don't give a child a task that is too difficult for his skills or maturity. Don't expect perfection on the first attempts. Instead, encourage him as he makes progress. Gently correct his mistakes and give him more only when he is ready.

3 **Be patient.** It is tempting to want him to hurry up and learn how to vacuum so that you can get on with our own personal agenda. But this isn't how children learn. Patient instruction is the best teacher. If you're in a hurry for him to do it right the first time he tries, then you've chosen the wrong time to demand it of him.

4 **Encourage them.** Your children want to help you and they long for your approval. Keep your words to them positive and uplifting. You are their first boss. Let the experience be a positive one.

5 **Model a good attitude.** This is most important for the long term. Our children echo the attitudes that we have. If we whine and complain about how much we hate cleaning the bathrooms or doing the laundry, then they will feel the same way about them. If we model cheerfulness, we are teaching them what good attitudes

look like. This has the potential for making an unpleasant task a more pleasant one. Good attitudes from everyone will also make your home happier.

6 **Give yourself grace.** You know your children better than anyone else. You know what they can handle, what's impossible and what is doable. Focus on your family's standards only, not what the parents in the neighbourhood are doing or what your in-laws have to say.

## Workshop

Take time to sit down with your spouse or partner and determine your standard for every area of your household, if these issues have never been addressed. The following questions may be tough ones to answer and they certainly make take longer than ten minutes to complete.

Any changes you make in your home life as a result of answering these questions should go slowly. But if it means finding more time for you to write (and having a more organized, peaceful home), it's worth the effort.

### Food
- What are the non-negotiables in our diet? Answers could be: *gluten-free, whole grains, vegan.*
- What days of the week will always be when we cook and which ones will be when we order a takeaway or eat convenience food? Answers could be: *We will cook dinner Monday–Thursday, order pizza every Friday, go out on Saturdays and eat leftovers or a convenience food on Sundays.*
- When will we shop?
- When will we plan a menu?
- Who will clean up, and when?
- What will we do for breakfasts on weekdays? Saturdays? Sundays?
- What will we do for lunch?
- What will we have for snacks?

**Household cleanliness and order**

- What are the non-negotiables we have for daily maintenance? Answers could be: *All the dishes are washed, dried and put away. All school papers are filed. Bathrooms are tidied. Wooden floors are swept.*
- What are the non-negotiables for weekly maintenance? Answers could be: *Bathrooms are cleaned, living room dusted, carpet vacuumed, bedding washed, bins taken out.*
- What are the non-negotiables for monthly maintenance? Answers could be: *Skirting boards dusted, ceilings dusted, refrigerator cleaned.*
- When will we attend to daily maintenance tasks?
- When will we attend to weekly tasks?
- When will we attend to monthly tasks?
- Who in the family will be responsible for what tasks?

## Creating a schedule

Take ten minutes and write down all the obligations in your week. If it's helpful, create a spreadsheet or print a schedule to look at what hours in the day are committed to work, school and errands, etc. Block out enough time for sleep and for family and friends. Then commit to at least one ten-minute block per day to write. Can you find one? More than one?

## Speeding things up

Take ten minutes and think about all the chores listed in the previous exercise – ones that must be done on a regular basis. Can you speed them up and make them more efficient? Can you time yourself? Can you structure the necessity of these tasks in such a way that you can create more writing time? This may take a few days of observation to fully see how you are using your time. If you're stuck with this, ask for help. You may know an analytical person who would have insight on this that you don't have.

## Focus point

For additional resources on how to get more organized, read Marla Cilley's website flylady.net, David Allen's book *Getting Things Done* or *Organizing from the Inside Out* by Julie Morgenstern.

## Finding the time

Take ten minutes to look at the month ahead and consider where you can cut back on other commitments – like *not* signing up to organize a school event or *not* attending that social gathering. Then mark your time on your calendar to use that time to write. Can you find more time?

## Making a plan

Take ten minutes and list the people, such as family and co-workers, who will be the most affected by your decision to write regularly. Make a plan on how you will communicate your need to them. Be creative. If I did not have my computer in my kitchen, with the document open and fast typing skills, I wouldn't have been able to succeed. My family did their best to work with me; it wasn't perfect, but it was all I had.

## Key idea

If you encounter resistance, make sure to take time – longer than ten minutes if you must – to deal with this in the best way you can. Seek advice from a professional. Take your time. Dreams and relationships are an equally important part of our happiness and the tender care of each is worth the time and effort.

# The silver lining

Agatha Christie's quote at the beginning of this chapter is comforting. With practice, I found – and for some reason this was much easier when my hands were in hot, soapy water – that I could get a lot of writing done when I wasn't actually writing. My mind stayed on the story even though my fingers were busy doing something else. So, like Agatha Christie, I planned my book while I did the dishes (and other household chores). In those non-writing times, I developed my characters, worked out their relationship problems and reasoned their motivations. I found plot holes. I sculpted my novel without actually writing my novel. This became a habit and the more I practised writing my novel in my non-writing time, the easier it became for me.

I wondered whether Agatha Christie was on to something – she did, after all, become the best-selling novelist of all time, according to *The Guinness Book of World Records*. Her books have been translated into 103 languages and *And Then There Were None* has sold over 100 million copies, making her the best-selling mystery writer ever and that book one of the best-selling ever.

Then I watched a BBC *Horizon* documentary, "The Creative Brain: How Insight Works," which confirmed that this 'plan a book while you're doing the dishes' idea is backed up scientifically. (At the time of writing, this video is available on YouTube.) The programme claims that it is during times of rest, or monotonous tasks, that our brain is at its most active. Doing the dishes, or being distracted, is exactly what we should be doing if we want to be at our most creative.

In her book *The Creative Brain,* psychologist and Harvard University researcher Shelley H. Carson addresses, among other things, how we can maximize our creativity. On her blog, shelleycarson.com, she talks about distractions: 'If you are stuck on a problem, an interruption can force an "incubation period",' she says. In other words, a distraction may provide the break you need to disengage from a fixation on the ineffective solution. She also goes on to say, 'Mind wandering itself is associated with highly creative people.'

## R. Keith Sawyer, *Explaining Creativity: The Science of Innovation*

*'Many people believe creativity comes in a sudden moment of insight and that this magical burst of an idea is a different mental process from our everyday thinking. But extensive research has shown that when you're creative, your brain is using the same mental building blocks you use every day – like when you figure out a way around a traffic jam.'*

Activities like doing the dishes don't require cognitive focus. These researchers are suggesting that, during mindless activities, our brains are free to relax and play around with the problems we suffered through earlier. This may also explain why a hot shower is a great place in which to get ideas. In a relaxing, comfortable, solitary place, like a shower, distractions are minimized and your subconscious can come to life. If you've had the pleasure of coming up with a great idea in the shower, it was because your prefrontal cortex (the place in your brain where you make decisions) and your default mode network (the part of your brain that is activated when you are completely at rest) worked together to make creative connections. Also, while you're in the shower, or have your hands in a sinkful of soapy dishes, the neurotransmitter dopamine is released into your brain. Dopamine can boost creativity, triggering alpha waves. Alpha waves are the active and energetic thought waves that help you communicate.

This theory, that rest and monotonous tasks stimulate creativity, was tested in the BBC documentary. Researchers sat down with volunteers and asked them to come up with creative uses for a brick. The researchers were looking for the most divergent ideas, the ones that demonstrated true insight and inspiration. After coming up with a few ideas, the volunteers rested for a bit; some did nothing for a few minutes, some participated in a mindless task, like sorting Lego, and others created a house from Lego using their creativity to solve a problem. Then the researchers asked them again to come up with uses for the brick. What happened next was surprising: the most divergent thinking came from the volunteers who had used their down time to do something mindless. It was as if their brain rested and recharged, but didn't stop altogether.

The suggested hypothesis was that, in order to be truly creative and maximize our time, we should find mindless tasks to do during our day (like wash the dishes) and work in short increments (like ten minutes) and then sit down with our plot, character or conflict problems and see what happens.

As a time-crunched writer, I found all of this fascinating and encouraging. I had thought that, since I didn't have a home office where I could shut the door, or much less an isolated cabin in the woods, like Annie Dillard or Henry David Thoreau, I was missing out. But according to the BBC, stopping and starting and doing housework *is better for my brain!* Perhaps Samuel Taylor Coleridge would have remembered his missing lines had he stooped to do housework, hoe the garden or wash the dog.

## Boost your creativity

Review the previous exercises and find a mindless task you must do on a regular basis – say, cleaning the kitchen after a meal. After you do that mindless activity, spend the next few minutes doing something creative. Make your activity a fun, simple one. Sketch, write a poem, build a Lego house, sculpt with Play-Doh, play a game of Scattergories, any occupation that requires you to be creative. Get your family involved. You don't need to spend a long time on this; ten minutes will do.

Now, write for ten minutes about this experience. Do you think that you were more creative or less? Did you find that ideas flowed freely? If you did this with your family, did you find it enjoyable?

## Watch The Creative Brain

Watch the BBC documentary The Creative Brain: How Insight Works. If it isn't on YouTube, you will be able to find it in a Google search. It's 55 minutes long, which goes past our ten-minute increment rule, but it's well done and encouraging.

Then take ten minutes to write down your insights or thoughts about this video and how you think you could apply these theories to your creative life.

# Where to next?

*The next chapter explains how to prepare for writing by creating a space and assembling the equipment you will need before you start.*

# 3

# Creating your space

What does a novelist look like? Perhaps the reality is neither as dramatic nor as romantic as the image of the writer frowning over a keyboard that is often portrayed in film or on television. The reality is that writers prepare first: they play around with words, they collect notes and they refer to other things they have written. Before they start to write, they have crafted their characters' appearance, quirks and motivations. They have researched their settings. They know the expectations of their genre. They may have an outline that they will follow, at least for a while. They have realized that the drafting of a novel requires organization and preparation.

This chapter addresses those preparations before you begin your novel writing journey. By the end of this chapter, you will be all the more prepared to begin your novel with far less frustration than the image above suggests.

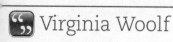

# Virginia Woolf

*'A woman must have money and a room of her own if she is to write fiction.'*

From movies or television, you may have seen the stereotypical image of a writer sitting at a typewriter with a stack of blank paper next to him on one side and an overflowing wastepaper basket on the other. He is usually frustrated. He types a sentence, maybe two, and he chews on the end of his pencil, gnawing it in frustration. Then he rips the paper out of the carriage, crumples it up and throws it over his shoulder to add to the growing pile. He grabs another off the pile to his left, rolls it back into the typewriter and pecks out another sentence. Within a few seconds the whole process starts again.

This presumptive image is one, I'm guessing, that many non-writers have about what writers do. I've never actually sat in the same room as a writer to witness this, but the writers I know don't write this way. (Most of them are far more environmentally conscious and would gently place their used paper in a recycling bin.) Generally speaking, the whole concept of sitting down at a blank piece of paper and a typewriter, or a document on a screen, or even a blank legal pad, is not an accurate picture of how writers write.

## A place to write

Despite Ms Woolf's sociological leanings, she could have been referring to writers of both genders. Every writer, you included, needs a place to write and a way to organize notes.

Your writing place should be uniquely yours. It will come by accident, by convenience, by habit, by choice or by purchasing such items as hardware and software, pencil and computer, printers and chairs. Your space is *your* space, not to be shared. Even if it is only two square feet, a kitchen counter, a modified closet, your laptop on your bed, your notepad on your coffee table or the only available chair at the local coffee bar, this will be the place you come to when you are sculpting. This is the place where you will imagine, hem and haw, ruminate and blather, weep and exclaim, compose and delete, plod through word after word, second-guess yourself, rip up that sheet of paper out of your literal or figurative typewriter and scrunch it up in frustration and toss it, perhaps, into a bin.

Your place is permanent or portable. Your space is beautiful or austere. Your place looks over a scenic view or a bare wall. Your space is there to remind you that this is your time and this task is for you alone. Your space is the silent partner in this journey, the one that says, 'I'll show up for you if you sit down and do the work.'

- Stephen King started out writing on an undersized desk in a closet meant for laundry.
- Ian Fleming wrote on a cliff-side house overlooking a beach in Jamaica.
- Roald Dahl wrote seated in a wing-backed chair with all his notes within reach.
- Eudora Welty regularly visited her mother in a nursing home and used the time in the car to make notes.
- J.M. Barrie wrote *Peter Pan* on a private island.
- Jane Austen took her notes and documents with her around the house, finding quiet spaces in her busy home.
- Wallace Stevens wrote his poetry on small pieces of paper when he took his walks.
- Jack Kerouac wrote *On the Road* in one long scroll, perhaps so that he didn't have to put sheets of paper into his typewriter.
- Because James Joyce was nearly blind, he wrote lying in bed, on his stomach, dressed in white, with a large blue crayon.

While it must be said that the various locations from which these writers created didn't propagate their genius, what it did do was allow their genius to be free. Your creative space is your sacred space, a place where you search your soul for the sake of art.

## Plan where you will write

For the next ten minutes, plan where you will write. If you already have a desk, a cliff-side house or a private island, great! You're ready for the next chapter. But if you don't, then work to find a space. Spend at least ten minutes preparing this space, getting everything you need – good lighting, comfort if possible, few distractions, reliable hardware and software and privacy. Get all your supplies together – whether it's the correct writing application for your computer (this document was written on Pages on a MacBook Air), a Google.doc, enough yellow legal pads and sharp pencils, voice-to-text software, a dictating machine, a voice recorder or a big blue crayon and a long scroll, get it ready. Encourage everyone in your household to keep their hands out of your stuff. Then make an effort to keep this writing space your writing space only. Don't pile your space with bills, schoolwork or folded laundry. In order for this system to work efficiently and in order for you to take this project seriously, you need to respect your space.

If you are writing portably, like Jane Austen or Wallace Stevens, make adjustments — use your phone, a laptop or a small notebook. Create your space and use it.

## The system you use

Let's return to the frustrated writer from the movies. Those crumpled papers on the floor are also not a part of a writers' reality. I believe that a competent writer will *save* every idea and sentence until they are sure they don't need them any more. A more accurate picture is therefore of someone with a filing cabinet or a stack of folders or index cards or *something* to show that they had kept their notes together and prepared themselves for the actual drafting of their story.

An experienced writer understands that 50 to 80 per cent of the work he is going to do, before the actual drafting, will never be seen by the reader. So, if a novelist is going to do this advance preparation well, they are going to have to be organized.

Just as there are different ways to set up space, there are different ways to organize. Each system varies from author to author, and from book to book. The chapters in Part Three of this book are arranged logically and describe the primary elements of a novel. If you had no other system, fancy software, index cards or filing cabinet, you could start with each of these chapters' headings – either in a paper file or in a file on your computer. For each of these headings, keep all your exercises, all your notes and any research you might do. You will want to have easy access to them as you draft.

## APPS AND SOFTWARE

In reality, twenty-first-century writers won't have any idea of how to use a manual typewriter. Instead, they have technology – their laptops, iPads and smartphones. Instead of scrunched-up paper on the floor, they have their notes organized in apps and software. Writers are no longer bound to the desk; they can write with the tools in their pocket. With new technology literally in their hands, budding novelists can find easy ways to write on the go and stay even more organized than their literary ancestors.

Here are just a few of the many apps available to writers:

- **Aeon Timeline** is an app available for Mac or Windows that allows you to create your own timelines. As you write your story, you can use Aeon to see all the chronological events, in any time increment, in your story at once. Events can be linked with external files, images and other material. Aeon also makes calculations, provides fantasy timelines for a custom calendar and it also syncs to Scrivener.

- **Chapters** is an iPad app that acts like a journal. It allows you to create multiple notebooks within the app yet provides common word-processing features, like timestamps, autosave and a word count. Journals can be exported or created into a .pdf for editing and publishing purposes. And a search feature allows you to find anything easily.

- **Dragon Dictation** is speech recognition software that takes your words and converts them to text. This could have many applications for people who have trouble typing. Dragon Dictation is fast and accurate, and is available for Windows or Mac.

- **Evernote** is an application for iPhones, iPads and computers that organizes all notes, documents, web clips, audio clips, image — anything you want to save. A search feature allows for easy access to everything you've saved. The sync feature ensures that all your devices have the same files. The Evernote online tutorials are easy to understand and setting up your book ideas is a painless process. Evernote also has several other compatible apps that can keep you organized.

- **Index Card** is an app that looks like index cards on a corkboard. You can compile ideas on separate cards, organizing them in any way you want, change the colour, use for multiple projects, track word counts and use long text fields for extended writing. Index Card is available for iPad.

- **My Writing Nook** is a web-based writing application, running on Google's app cloud, whose purpose is to create a clutter-free writing environment. It has easy access to a dictionary and thesaurus and provides a word count. It's free and is available for all computers, iPad, iPhone and Android.

- **Pomodoro Time Management** is a method of working in chunks of time divided by breaks, developed in the 1980s. By using the app (or even buying the red tomato kitchen timer that the technique was named after), you can break down your daily tasks into small increments of time to maximize productivity. So, as a ten-minute novelist, you could find the app helpful in meeting your goals.

- **Scapple** is a mind-mapping app that helps organize thoughts and ideas. According to their own description, 'It's more like a freeform text editor that allows you to make notes anywhere on the page and to connect them using straight lines or arrows. If you've ever scribbled down ideas all over a piece of paper and drawn lines between related thoughts, then you already know what Scapple does.' Because it is compatible with Scrivener (see below), this app can be useful for writers as they begin their brainstorming or observing. It's available for Mac and Windows.

- **Scrivener** is a popular content generation tool used by novelists, screenwriters, researchers and anyone who has to write, organize and research a long document. Scrivener has many features that allow writers to keep track of plotlines, characters and notes. It is one of the more expensive writing tools on this list, but well worth the money to have such flexible and thorough software. Scrivener is available for Mac and Windows and commonly used by creative professionals.

- **Write or Die** is a web-based application for Windows, Mac or Linux that allows writers to set specific goals, such as increments of time or a specific word count. Write or Die then offers positive visual or audio stimulation if you meet that goal. If you don't meet the goal, then a negative consequence will occur. Writers customize what types of rewards and consequences they want. Write or Die is a fresh approach to accountability and can obviously improve productivity.

These are only some of the hundreds of apps available for writers. Regardless of how you write, it is critical that you spend your time on your notes and drafts as efficiently as possible. Find what works for you.

## Key idea

You are a writer. These are the tools for your journey. You will not succeed without them.

## Plan your filing system

For the next ten minutes, plan your filing system. If you want, create files that correspond to the following story elements. These match specific chapters in the book. As you progress through the exercises, you can keep your notes here. If you don't have what you need – software, apps or paper files on hand – then get it as soon as possible.

The story elements covered in Parts three and four of this book are as follows:

- Plot
- Genre
- World building
- The protagonist
- Additional characters
- The antagonist
- The narrator and point of view
- The three-act structure
- Sequences, scenes and beats
- Dialogue
- Opening lines and hooks
- Drafting

## Where to next?

*Part Two,* Thinking like a writer, *is about how you can transform your own rich life experience into material for your novel, especially at the beginning stages, and the next chapter will help you organize what you know into a story world with universal resonance.*

# PART TWO

## Thinking like a writer

# 4

## 'Write what you know'

The adage 'Write what you know', often attributed to Mark Twain, is mostly about expressing universal truths rather than relating specific life experiences. If writers are truly honest and tap into their own deep well of experiences, they captivate their readers by drawing them into their rich world, just as Twain did in his books.

Like Twain, your job as a writer is to make the experience of reading your story as authentic as possible: authentic at the narrative, descriptive and emotional levels. If you can somehow catalogue your experiences, especially in the beginning stages of novel sculpting, then perhaps you may be inspired to express them honestly. Regardless of your genre choice, your own rich life should be the first place to start when you begin a novel. The purpose of this chapter is to help you organize what you know so that you can include those telling details.

Victoria Mixon, *The Art and Craft of Fiction*

> *'There is no question that a really good writer – someone who's earned the name – writes about what they know. That knowledge is the source of all telling detail.'*

In *The Adventures of Tom Sawyer* and *Huckleberry Finn*, Twain wrote about life along the Mississippi River, allowing his readers to experience Hannibal, Missouri and the late nineteenth century through the eyes of two lively boys. His world was an authentic one, not just in the facts – which were similar to those of his childhood – but also in the feelings that it aroused in its readers.

Write what you know because:

- you have an intimate knowledge of your life, your hobbies, your interests and your pursuits
- you have seen what your readers haven't seen
- there are details in your life your readers have never considered
- you are tapping into the universal truths within your life's experiences.

## Workshop

This workshop will take several ten-minute sessions, perhaps one for each item in the list below. As you find the time, write as much as you can about the following subjects, going back as far in your memory as possible. Write a note, a sentence, or an anecdote – whatever it takes to have you remember details. Each item starts with the simple basics of your life and progresses into the more intimate, and potentially more difficult, details. It is in the later sections, if you are truly honest, where you will be tapping into your humanity. It is this humanity that will endear you to your readers. You must not neglect these later sections, as difficult as they are. This exercise has no specific end point, so finish when you feel you have enough information.

| | |
|---|---|
| 1 Places I've lived | 18 Employers |
| 2 Jobs I've had | 19 Teachers |
| 3 Schools I've attended | 20 Other memorable people |
| 4 Things I've studied | 21 Pets |
| 5 Activities and hobbies | 22 Moments of embarrassment |
| 6 Organizations | 23 Moments of failure |
| 7 Specific life events | 24 Moments of success |
| 8 Holidays | 25 Moments of pride |
| 9 Trips | 26 Moments of pain |
| 10 Favourite pop culture (music, film, books, TV) | 27 Moments of trauma |
| 11 Favourite foods | 28 Moments of secrecy |
| 12 Favourite rooms | 29 Moments of fear |
| 13 Favourite items of clothing | 30 Moments of crisis |
| 14 Other favourite possessions | 31 Moments of joy |
| 15 Friends | 32 Moments of humour |
| 16 Crushes or romantic partners | 33 Moments of sorrow |
| 17 Family members | |

This is not an exhaustive list. If you think of other things to add to it, please do. *What you know* is vitally important to your art, so don't allow the insufficiencies of this list to hold you back.

Save your notes in your newly created filing system. You may be using it for future exercises and later drafting.

The result of this exercise is that you will have a vast collection of inspiration. Return to these files as you draft.

# The universal human struggle

First Mark Twain says, 'Write what you know' and he graces the world with the brilliant *Tom Sawyer* and *Huckleberry Finn,* and then what does he do? He writes what he doesn't know. He wrote about a doppelgänger pair during the time of Henry VIII in *The Prince and the Pauper.* He fought the English with *Joan of Arc.* He brought his audience into a fantasy with *A Connecticut Yankee in King Arthur's Court.* Throughout all his books, he proved that he could believably and brilliantly write about lives and times far from post-Civil War Missouri.

Yet, in these later, more fantastic stories, regardless of what the critics or public thought, Twain's characters faced injustice after injustice, they found comfort when they were rescued, they held on to hope till the end. His readers identified with his creations, not because of the settings or the details, but because of the universal human struggle. Twain used his imagination, his own passions, his apparent love of history and research and risked the unfamiliar to tell some great stories.

 ## Mark Twain

*'Reality can be beaten with enough imagination.'*

Perhaps we should follow Twain's example and write about what we don't know – in order to tell what we do know. The stories that we write that are outside our own worlds, outside of *what we know,* perhaps even in the genres of fantasy and science fiction, can be the vehicles to fully tell what we *do* know about current issues, current conflicts and current societal demands.

As Twain discovered, it's risky. When we *write what we don't know*, we are moving from the familiar to the more novel world of storytelling. Once we step into that world, we can't take our authentic experiences, our observations or our sentiment into the world with us unless those things submit to the needs of the story.

Writing what you don't know is harder. Writers who are not afraid to write what they don't know must be willing to fight with meaning and clarity; they must be willing to research or sculpt the world they want to create. They must convince their readers to come along for the ride. Unfortunately for Twain, his critics at the time didn't think the risk was worth it. Perhaps his 'passengers' on his previous literary journeys were expecting Becky Thatcher.

## Robert McKee, *Story: Substance, Structure, Style and the Principles of Screenwriting*

'A storyteller is a life poet, an artist who transforms day-to-day living, inner life and outer life, dream and actuality into a poem whose rhyme scheme is events rather than words – a two-hour metaphor that says: Life is like this! Therefore, a story must abstract from life to discover its essences, but not become an abstraction that loses all sense of life-as-lived. A story must be like life, but not so verbatim that it has no depth or meaning beyond what's obvious to everyone on the street.'

Everything you will do in the remainder of this book will be about how you will submit your words and your world to the story. The story, *your* story, is a brutal taskmaster. It will insist that you remain true to *story*, regardless of your need for sentimentality or self-indulgence. You, as its creator, must not tolerate the minutiae, the distracting, the uninteresting, the discordant or impure. In order to meet this objective, you will, at times, be forced to discard what you know and dig deeper. You may have to change a perspective, edit brutally or omit your favourite passages altogether.

This means that all the notes you made in the last section of this book may not fit into your story. That dialogue you wrote down from yesterday is probably too inane. The memory from your childhood may be too sentimental. The great anecdote that you told over the water cooler may be just that – a cute story, but not one to consider novel worthy. You may have to exaggerate your antagonist to be far more than what you remember your Home Economics teacher to be. You may have to accelerate the events surrounding that car accident to make it more interesting and more emotional. You may have to concentrate that dialogue down to its core meaning to make it fit into the scene. You may have to twist, cajole, invert, stretch, pound or flatten what you *know* to make it what you *don't know*.

But this is where your imagination takes over. As a story-maker, you can create anything, you can be anybody, you can live in any historical time period, you can be anyone you want, you can love anyone you want, you can fight and kill anyone you want. You can be saint or sinner, hero or villain, loved or despised, silly or sublime. You have the power to do and be *anything*.

## Make some lists

Make an exhaustive list of every career or job that has fascinated you. Then make a long list of every city you've ever wanted to visit or live in. Make a list, similar to a 'bucket list', of any activity, hobby or experience that you've always wanted to try.

Now list ten specific types of people that are as far removed from you as they could possibly be, either in socio-economic status, education, geography, time or interests. For example, I am a white, college-educated, middle-aged mother living in New England in the early twenty-first century. On my list I could put, for example:

- a Puerto Rican gang member living in Los Angeles in 1970
- a Geisha girl from 1930s Japan
- an eight-year-old boy, an orphan, left alone on the Kansas prairie in 1875
- a Roman emperor
- a lady-in-waiting at Queen Elizabeth I's court.

Put all these lists in a file. Later you may well find inspiration from them to explore a new world.

## Rewrite an anecdote

Choose one anecdote you wrote for the workshop in this chapter. Now rewrite it, exaggerating each element of the story, the characters, the dialogue, the action, the setting. Once you are done with it, evaluate the story objectively. Is it more interesting? Does it have more meaning? What do you think of the changes?

## Where to next?

*The next chapter will show you how to develop your own unique writing voice, through reading, observation and the technique of free writing.*

# 5

# Finding your voice

It is 'voice' that carries the most artistic weight of our storytelling. All my children could retell the story of *The Three Bears* but they would all do it differently, according to their different talents, skills and personality. If I were to pick the most appealing version, I would choose one over the others on the basis of style, specific word choices, mood and sheer talent all mixed up together. This distinction in their storytelling is *voice*.

Voice is not something that can be taught or learned, unlike technical skills such as grammar and spelling. The most successful novelists are those who have developed their own unique voice by being open to various influences, from reading and observing the world around them and then practising, often using a technique called free writing. If you are to write a marketable novel, you will need to develop a unique voice too.

## Billy Collins

*'You come by your style by learning what to leave out. At first you tend to overwrite – embellishment instead of insight. You either continue to write puerile bilge, or you change. In the process of simplifying oneself, one often discovers the thing called voice.'*

A writer's voice is like good wine. The complexities of a wine's taste come from a variety of sources – the grapes, the climate of the vineyard, the type of barrel it was stored in, the chemical composition of the soil and the techniques of the winemaker. Wine is complicated.

Just like wine, a writer's voice is a complex creation influenced by many different things. The best writers, like the best wine, have spent time developing their essence into something distinctive. The best writers, like the best wine, need to be savoured and enjoyed and appreciated for their uniqueness. I also think that writers who take the time to develop their voice are like the winemaker who tinkers with all the factors that make his wine stand out from others.

On his blog, literary agent Chip MacGregor said that the thing that he looks for most in new writers is an original voice. But how to get one is somewhat mysterious: voice is not something that can be taught or learned in a class, unlike technical writing skills like grammar and spelling. You can go to a conference and learn the newest marketing tricks, but you can't go to one and come back with a spectacular voice. The most successful novelists are those who are comfortable with themselves in their storytelling. If you are to write a marketable novel, you will need a unique voice too.

# Reading

So how does our voice develop? Like wine, I'd like to suggest beginning novelists tinker with influences. Like the winemaker, I say that, to develop voice, you need to nurture the right kind of environmental factors. While it sounds rather attractive to sit in a barrel for months and do nothing but write, I think a more practical way to develop voice is to surround ourselves with rich words. By finding great examples of voice and studying them, savouring them and then recreating them, our own voice becomes more flavourful, distinct and palatable.

Here's how:

- **Read non-Western writers.**
  As a white, Anglo-Saxon Protestant living in the most white, Anglo-Saxon Protestant part of the USA, I have found that leaving my literary comfort zone is enlightening and adventurous. My suggestions would be *That Thing around Your Neck* by African writer Chimamanda Adichie, *White Tiger* by Indian writer Aravind Adiga and *Crescent* by Middle Eastern writer Diana Abu-Jaber. Reading these beautiful books was good for me on many levels. It will be good for you too.

- **Read avant-garde(-ish) works.**
  Some books are creative to the point of being annoying, but some innovative books can provide new literary experiences that can stretch our mind. Often these books are hard to categorize, or they're critics' favourites. These are the types of books that I admire not just for their distinctive voice but also because of the courage it took to do something different in storytelling. (Kudos to not just the writer but to the publishers who believed in them!) My suggestions would be *The Selected Works of T.S. Spivet* by Reif Larsen, *The Girl Who Circumnavigated Fairyland in a Ship of Her Own Making* by Catherynne M. Valente, and *The Curious Incident of the Dog in the Night-time* by Mark Haddon.

- **Read twentieth-century greats.**
  Spend some time getting to know the notable literary voices of the twentieth century: the list includes Flannery O'Connor, F. Scott Fitzgerald, Ernest Hemingway, John Steinbeck, C.S. Lewis, George Orwell, James Joyce and D.H. Lawrence. These writers are a part of our literary heritage for a reason. They worked hard at their distinctive voices and as a result shaped our culture and our literary landscape. It is a good idea, when reading these authors, to keep notes, write out great sentences, memorize passages and savour their words.

- **Read and memorize poetry.**

  If you spend time swimming around with good poetry from any time period, you will be playing with metaphor, rhythm, imagery, description, structure and voice in small, bite-size packages. Don't know where to start? Go to PoemHunter.com and sign up for their daily email poem. Then read it. Choose a poet to study – one a month or so – and read it aloud, allowing the words and rhythms to dance with your tongue and woo your soul. This will, undoubtedly, affect your writing voice. And if you have children, you could make this a family project, to memorize poetry. Our favourites include 'Charge of the Light Brigade' by Alfred, Lord Tennyson, 'If' by Rudyard Kipling, and anything by Jack Prelutsky, Robert Louis Stevenson or William Blake.

Like wine, good writing is complicated. Like wine, good writing from a distinctive voice can be a beautiful, toast-worthy work of art.

## Read more

Spend ten minutes considering how you can read more during your day to develop your voice. Choose a book from the above list or from another source. Plan to read (either a regular book or an ebook or listen to an audiobook) for at least ten minutes a day.

## Free write

After reading for ten minutes, do a ten-minute free write about what you read. Were you inspired? Do you have insight about this exercise?

# Becoming observant

## Flannery O'Connor

*'The writer should never be ashamed of staring. There is nothing that does not require his attention.'*

Between the world of what we are familiar with (what we know) and the world that is completely imaginary (what we don't know), there could, potentially, be items, people or settings that so move, inspire, amuse or fascinate us that we want to remember them. The best writers are those who are not only keen observers of the world they are in and of the people they encounter, but also record keepers: they note down what they see, file it away and save it for the sculpting of their novels.

## Victoria Mixon, *The Art and Craft of Fiction*

*'This world must be visible. It needs specific light and dark, scenes, sights, and objects with shapes and sizes and colours. It must be audible. It needs sounds and silence, voices and a lack of voices. It must be tangible, with textures and temperatures, tastes and smells, bodily experiences and the absence of them. It must be a real place. You are here to record that real place.'*

Just as an artist might carry a sketchbook around with him, sketching what he sees, a writer must be in the habit of observing the world and writing about it. A good writer notices details and then uses his words to communicate sensations, emotions, sentiment, symbolism and metaphor. With a thorough description, a writer can add value to what he observes. The reader cannot only see what he sees, but see how the object described plays a part in the greater story. The item described may be something on a desk, the murder weapon or the victim's sandwich. Descriptions may also be of a person or a place, allowing readers to 'see' what the writer sees and attach themselves emotionally to the words written. As you will later sculpt your novel, you will need to be able to capture appearances and descriptions. Practising now will make it easier later.

Only through good observational skills can fresh and vibrant descriptions be written. This section explores how to stop and *stare*, as Flannery O'Connor says. Perhaps we should be still and look. Perhaps listen. Perhaps taste and touch.

## LOOKING MORE CLOSELY

Writers need to be in the habit of looking closely at objects. Objects are the 'props' of our stories and it is the rare novel that has no need of a handgun, a knife, a jewel, an animal, someone's wallet, a faded photograph or something else that helps tell the story. An item well described can add layers of history, value, meaning and symbolism to the plot.

Writers also need to routinely watch people. So much of a person's character and story is told on their face, by what they are wearing, how they hold themselves or what they are doing. When you observe people and put their nuances into your stories, you are tapping into hidden conflicts, personality quirks, traits and motivations. You can find inspiration in their gestures and movements.

Writers also need to take in every detail in a setting, such as a room, or a sports field or an office. A thorough description of a setting has the power to set mood, underscore conflicts and create the details of a great scene. The more you describe, the more detail you convey and the more intimately you understand the world, the more likely it is that your novel will be interesting, fresh and rich.

## How to look

The first step in observing is using the five senses. Writers who are thorough in writing about colours, shapes and textures, using clear descriptors and vibrant nouns, can accurately create an object in a reader's mind. But there is more to an object that what is seen. A skilled writer can also describe what sounds the object makes, what it smells or even tastes like, or what it feels like in the palm of one's hand.

Next, a skilled writer can expand beyond the obvious. Like a real-life Sherlock Holmes, a writer asks questions that would include the '5Ws and an H' (Who? What? When? Where? Why? and How?) – *Why is this item here? What is its purpose? What is its value, both sentimental and practical? Who would want it? Why would they have it? What could an observer know about the person who owns it?*

> Similar questions can be asked of people: *What do they appear to want? What do they really want? What is keeping them from gaining it? How are they related to the people around them? How are they feeling? What is their social status? Their economic status? What kind of education did they have?*
>
> Even a setting can be described through questions. *How do all the people here relate to one another? What is the mood? Where are the conflicts? What are the values here? Who belongs here? Who doesn't?*

Observation takes practice, so always keep a notebook handy, to jot down what you notice or what interests you and then file it away for the future composition.

This is what I observed the week I wrote this chapter. Last week, at a civic club function a man came to the podium to review announcements. The man was of average height. He had a headful of milky white hair and his pale face was devoid of expression. His shirt was a beige and he wore khaki pants. All his clothes were wrinkled. When he came to the microphone, he stammered and coughed. He hesitated and said, 'Um'. His monotone was as colourless as his visual impression. He didn't seem to put himself in his announcements, but mumbled and rambled with little passion and little energy. He was memorable in that he had so little colour, both literally and figuratively.

This left an impression on me. I wrote a note on my phone so that I could remember it. I did stare, just as Flannery O'Connor suggested, but since everyone was also looking at him, my staring wasn't obvious.

## Write about an object

Choose an item from your home or office that is smaller than your hand. The best choice would be an item that has more than one colour, more than two sides, more than one texture, and more than one use. Place it near your writing space and write as much as you can about this item in ten minutes.

1 Start with your senses. Describe what you see and feel with this item. Then move on to other sensations. Does it make a noise you can describe? Does it have a taste or smell?

2 As a journalist would, write the 5W and H questions about this item. *What is it used for? Where did it come from? Who would own an item like this? Where would they get it? How would it come into their possession? Why would one have an item such as this? What would you learn about the person who owns it?*

## Write about a person

Choose a photo of a family or a group of friends from the Awkward Family Photos website or something from a magazine or Google images. Write for ten minutes about everything that you see in the photo, starting with the senses and then moving on to the deeper questions, especially about the relationships in the photo.

## Observing people and places

1 Spend a half-hour or longer in a public setting. This could be at your local coffee shop, in the break room at work or on a bench near foot traffic. Choose five people and spend ten minutes each describing and observing them, writing down everything you see, creating possible conflicts and motivations. Be a Sherlock Holmes and see whether you can determine facts about them from any clues.

2 Choose a room with several people in it. This can be a restaurant setting, a work environment, a school event, a pubic space, as long as it is enclosed. Write for ten minutes describing the room itself, all of the sights and sounds that can observe and then describe the actions and relationships between the people in that setting.

## DESCRIPTIVE WRITING

Read the following examples of good description from some of my favourite books. As you read these, pay attention to what it is that gets the most description from the writer. What kinds of emotion are stirred in you when you read each passage? Look at the more vivid words, especially the adjectives and verbs and consider how your own word choices in the previous exercises could be just as vivid.

*Slowly the golden memory of the dead sun fades from the hearts of the cold, sad clouds. Silent, like sorrowing children, the birds have ceased their song, and only the moorhen's plaintive cry and the harsh croak of the corncrake stirs the awed hush around the couch of waters, where the dying day breathes out her last.*

Jerome K. Jerome, *Three Men in a Boat* (Penguin Books, 1989 [1889])

*The brambles and the thorns grew thick and thicker in a ticking thicket of bickering crickets. Farther along and stronger, bonged the gongs of a throng of frogs, green and vivid on their lily pads. From the sky came the crying of flies, and the pilgrims leaped over a bleating sheep creeping knee-deep in a sleepy stream, in which swift and slippery snakes slid and slithered silkily, whispering sinful secrets.*

James Thurber, *The 13 Clocks* (Yearling, 1950)

*And so I may tell you that the leaves began to turn red as September and her friends rushed through the suddenly cold air on their snorting, roaring highwheels, and you might believe me. But no red you have ever seen could touch the crimson bleed of the trees in that place. No oak gone gnarled and orange with October is half as bright as the bough that bent over September's hue—I woke to the sound of the knock on the door and sat up in the light from the neon sign that snaked along the wall outside the window. An empty carton of moo goo gai pan sat beside me: I hadn't thrown it out.*

Catherynne M. Valente, *The Girl Who Circumnavigated Fairyland in a Ship of Her Own Making* (Feiwel & Friends, 2011)

*Mr Shiflet stopped just inside the yard and set his box on the ground and tipped his hat at her as if she were not in the least afflicted; then he turned toward the old woman and swung the hat all the way off. He had long black slick hair that hung flat from a part in the middle to beyond the tips of his ears on either side. His face descended in forehead for more than half its length and ended suddenly with his features just balanced over a jutting steel-trap jaw. He seemed to be a young man but he had a look of composed dissatisfaction as if he understood life thoroughly.*

Flannery O'Connor, 'The Life You Save May Be Your Own', in *A Good Man Is Hard to Find* (Harcourt, Brace & Co., 1955)

*We sat in the back of the long room filled with black folding chairs, so still you could hear the old ladies fanning themselves. Dry coughs and solemn whispers, and faint odors of flowers and mothballs. Men in their blue Sunday suits. They walked softly, hardly letting their feet touch the floor. When Mr. Lundberg shut the lid on Aunt May, he did it as if she were made of spun glass and might shatter.*

Garrison Keillor, *Lake Wobegon Days* (Viking Penguin, 1985)

*The next day was rainy and dark. Rain fell on the roof of the barn and dripped steadily from the eaves. Rain fell in the barnyard and ran in crooked courses down in to the lane where thistles and pigweed grew. Rain spattered against Mrs Zuckerman's kitchen windows and came gushing out of the downspouts. Rain fell on the backs of the sheep as they grazed in the meadow. When the sheep tired of standing in the rain, they walked slowly up the lane and into the fold.*

E.B. White, *Charlotte's Web* (Harper Collins, 1952)

*Mr Dub didn't look like much. He didn't look like the kind of man to raise a fist to the city bully. His skinny legs hid inside wide-legged trousers, bent at the knee from wear. His shirts bloomed around him. He might have been sturdier after the war, but his face was vaguely hollow, like a shrunken jack o'lantern. Gaunt, Mama called him. Gaunt described Mr Dub exactly: dried up by the war, and boiled down to the base of his person. He only said words he meant to say, and he did everything with a calm purpose. He might have seemed weird to others. People want noise and laughter and happiness. Mr. Dub could do noise and laughter and happiness, but it was quieter, almost mechanical. Only the warm, browned butter eyes said he was genuine.*

Jennifer Perrine Luitweiler,
*Seven Days in May* (Createspace, 2014)

# The free writing technique

I have one writing tool that I use almost daily. This tool moves me from the nebulous mess of an idea to some sort of draft. This tool has taught me to write fast and it is the best defence against my inner critic. This tool surprises me with what I come up with and it moves me forward, as I draft, more effectively than any other tool. This tool is the *free write*.

A free write is an unfiltered and unstructured spew of words on paper. It is loose, sloppy and free. It has as little self-correction as possible. It works best for people like me who are already on the speedy side when it comes to writing. In the free write, convention is thrown out of the window and spelling and grammar are ignored (unless you choose not to ignore them). Being correct takes a back seat to being free.

## Stephen King

*'Writing is magic, as much the water of life as any other creative art. The water is free. So drink. Drink and be filled up.'*

From free writes, new insights can be discovered. Great metaphors can be identified. In a free write, a memory can be triggered and new depth can be expressed. In a free write, the full richness of conscious and subconscious life can pour out on to the page.

The free write is much like potter's clay. It is just a hunk of material, not the art itself. From this unrefined mass, true craftsmanship begins. A skilled writer/craftsman can take the raw material of this free write and shape it into something amazing. He can analyse it from all sides, move sentences around and chip away word after word, substituting vibrant verbs and descriptive nouns.

By practising free writing, a writer will
- have far less writer's block
- be stimulated by other ideas
- use his designated writing time wisely.
- have silenced inner critics faster
- have strengthened individual voice
- have raised the standard of excellence
- have trusted in the creative process
- become more confident
- be released from the expectations of others
- become a better writer.

## Workshop

If you have never attempted a free write before, this is how you do it.
- Open up a new document or a grab a piece of paper.
- Set a timer for ten minutes.
- Write *everything* you can about any subject you want (refer to the list in the workshop for Chapter 4 if you need a prompt) as fast as you can. Include every nuance, every tangent, every cliché, every thought, everything. Think stream of consciousness or a Jackson Pollock painting. Just write it down!
- Don't stop for anything – especially that little voice inside you that says you must be doing it wrong.

- Read what you have written but have low, low expectations. Do not be surprised if, after ten minutes of free writing, you have only one or two sentences you can work with. You are not looking for good sentences but for good concepts, good metaphors and good description. You are looking for good art. You are looking for the unusual. You are looking for the phrase that is more *you* than anything else. You are looking for your distinctive voice.

As you progress in the development of the elements of your novel, you will find that free writing will enhance the sculpting process. Free write your themes. Free write your characters. Free write your settings. Free write at every single step in the course of writing. No one is looking, so let go of every hindrance and keep going. The most authentic, passionate, creative writers are those who have tapped into this part of who they are and have written freely. You need to learn to do this.

I believe that it is in the practice of the free write that brilliant ideas are conceived. I believe that it is only in free writing that the other muscles, like analysis, organization and metaphor really come to play. I believe that good writers are good free writers.

## Where to next?

*Part Three systematically explains how to build each of the elements that make up a story within the classical story structure. The next chapter covers how to make a plot from your story idea.*

# PART THREE

## THREE

Sculpting the elements
of story

# 6

## Story and plot

You are working through this book so that you can develop the skills to write a novel that will tell a story and stir the emotions of your readers. The *story* is the life of the novel. With a powerful, emotionally well-thought-out story, your readers can be stirred to a whole range of feelings. Your readers can be challenged. *Your readers can be changed.*

The *story* itself is distinctively different from the *novel*. The *story* is the narrative – what happens, who it happens to and what happens in the end. The *novel* is the vehicle in which it is presented, the form in which the story takes place.

Since the beginning of the Western storytelling tradition, stories have had plots. Your job as a storyteller is to invite your reader on an emotional ride. By choosing a plot, you are giving them clues about what to expect.

# Key idea

In the chapters in this section, covering the elements of story, including plot, genre, characters, dialogue and three-act structure, you will see how your current ideas fit classical story structure. Once you have carefully sculpted each element of your story according to your vision, you will be ready to write your novel.

# Robert McKee, *Story: Substance, Structure, Style and the Principles of Screenwriting*

*'Our appetite for story is a reflection of the profound human need to grasp the patterns of living, not merely as an intellectual exercise, but within a very personal, emotional experience.'*

FRODO: *I can't do this, Sam.*

SAM: *I know. It's all wrong. By rights we shouldn't even be here. But we are. It's like in the great stories, Mr Frodo. The ones that really mattered. Full of darkness and danger, they were. And sometimes you didn't want to know the end. Because how could the end be happy? How could the world go back to the way it was when so much bad had happened? But in the end, it's only a passing thing, this shadow. Even darkness must pass. A new day will come. And when the sun shines it will shine out the clearer. Those were the stories that stayed with you. That meant something, even if you were too small to understand why. But I think, Mr Frodo, I do understand. I know now. Folk in those stories had lots of chances of turning back, only they didn't. They kept going. Because they were holding on to something.*

FRODO: *What are we holding on to, Sam?*

SAM: *That there's some good in this world, Mr Frodo … and it's worth fighting for.*

*The Two Towers* (Dir. Peter Jackson, New Line Cinema, 2002)

I've watched the film *The Two Towers* several times, once in the cinema and then again, at home, every two years or so, in my living room. During one of these home viewings, I was sprawled on the couch, miserable. I was pregnant, suffering from hypertension, and emotional. In addition to my health being precarious, my personal life was facing a severe trial too. All I thought about were my problems, which didn't help my hypertension at all. When I watched this film, and viewed the section with Sam and Frodo resting on the cliffs on the way to Mordor, I was *with* them. I felt their despair. Like Frodo, I wanted to give up too.

But Sam's words stirred something in me. I probably cried during this scene because I was exhausted and fearful, but I also cried because I recognized Frodo's suffering; I could feel it. I was drawn to, comforted by and responsive to the *story itself*. My courage was built up. I wept and snuggled closer to my husband and concluded that somehow I, too, would get through this. (I did. We had our own happy ever after.)

This story – the story Sam told Frodo, the story of *The Two Towers* and the way the director Peter Jackson told this story – moved me by its power, its comfort and its truth. To this day, I cannot watch that scene without thinking of my own personal struggle and how I conquered my fear through Sam's words. For me, Tolkien's original story has now transcended the novel and the film and now is a part of me, because *the story changed me*.

## Novel and story

Consider the difference between a novel and a story. Have you thought about this distinction before? Does this change what you accomplish with this book?

*The Two Towers* is the novel of the story of how Frodo and Sam travelled to Mordor after the Fellowship of the Ring broke up. The film *The Two Towers* is a cinematic interpretation of this story. Good storytellers do not necessarily make good novelists, but a good novel most certainly has a good story in it. The most loved and most commercially successful novels are those that have followed the familiar patterns of what is known in Western civilization as a story. It's called classical story structure.

# Robert McKee, *Story: Substance, Structure, Style and the Principles of Screenwriting*

*'Classical design means a story built around an active protagonist who struggles against primarily external forces of antagonism to pursue his or her desire through continuous time, within a consistent and causally connected fictional reality, to a closed ending of absolute, irreversible change.'*

Most of the stories you have read, seen or heard in any format have followed McKee's definition. This is the generally most accepted form of storytelling in our culture, which means that your readers are used to classical stories too. Beginning novelists should learn the elements of it, master the concepts of it, and practise it continuously before trying anything that deviates from it.

## Analysing your story idea

Consider McKee's definition of story, quoted above. If you've tinkered around with your story idea already, write a paragraph about it. Does it touch every point that McKee makes in his definition? What's missing? Why?

Stories have the power to move and to transform. As we learn the elements of them – plots, genres, structures and conflicts – and as we develop rich, believable characters and put them in complex, interesting worlds, we'll be able to sculpt a story brilliantly. Perhaps our stories will be, as Sam Gamgee says, 'the ones that really matter'.

## Your favourite stories

Make a list of ten of your favourite stories – they can be films or TV shows, not just novels. What is it about them that you love? What emotions do you find yourself experiencing in them? Do you have anything that moved you the way that I was moved in *The Two Towers*?

## The emotions in your story

Do you have ideas already about what your novel's story is about?
If you do, make a list of all the emotions that you would like your
readers to experience in your story.

# Plot

## E.M. Forster

'We have defined a story as a narrative of events arranged in
their time-sequence. A plot is also a narrative of events, the
emphasis falling on causality.'

According to E.M. Forster, 'The king died and then the queen died'
is a story. 'The king died, and then the queen died of grief' is a plot.
While the story asks 'What happened?' the plot asks 'Why does it
happen?' By asking 'Why?' in the beginning of our novel sculpting,
you are choosing a category of story. This prepares your reader for
the emotional journey you are about to create. Even if you already
familiar with various common plots, it is good to review them.
Familiarizing yourself with how your specific plot works can help
you draft your story later.

If you want to coax your reader forward, have them trust you with
their emotions, join with you on the ride, then you need to align
your plot with general ideas that have been around for centuries. A
skilled novelist assures his reader that this adventure story will go
somewhere exciting, that the romance will be passionate and that
the mysteries will be solved.

Much has been written about the various plots in Western culture.
I've aligned to conventional wisdom by suggesting that there are
*seven*. The basic storyline of any story, no matter how complicated,
no matter the genre, style or setting, could, potentially, fall into one
or more of these seven plot categories. The definitive explanation of
these seven plot stories is in Christopher Booker's 2004 tome *The
Seven Basic Plots: Why We Tell Stories*. These seven will be familiar
to you. You've been reading or watching them your whole life.

# 1 Overcoming the monster

In this plot, the objective of the main character is to conquer the force that is attacking his homeland. Stories using this plot would include any monster movie; they can be as simple as *Godzilla* or as complex as *The Andromeda Strain* or *The War of the Worlds*. A skilled writer uses tense scenes to build suspense. He manipulates the story in such a way that a reader is never completely sure that the good guy will be victorious. The author must explain why the monster is so dangerous and why the main character is the only one that can do the overcoming. Most ancient Greek and Roman myths – those of Heracles, Perseus and Theseus, for example – fall into this category. More recent examples include *The Pushcart War, Of Mice and Men,* the Harry Potter series, *The Girl with the Dragon Tattoo, Jaws, The Andromeda Strain, A Tale of Two Cities, Dracula, Frankenstein, War of the Worlds,* and the James Bond stories.

# 2 The quest

These stories include adventure, discovery, rescue, escape, pursuit, voyage, or any type of story in which the main character has to travel from one place to another for any number of reasons. Often, quest stories include demonstrations of courage, determination, physical strength, cunning and victory. The author must fully explain *why* this goal is so important and *why* the journey is so difficult. If the main characters do not achieve the main goal, they are rewarded in some other way for their hard work. Examples of this include: *The Odyssey, The Lord of the Rings, Treasure Island, The Hunger Games, The Swiss Family Robinson, Dune, The Last Olympian, The Pilgrim's Progress, Don Quixote, The Call of the Wild, A Wrinkle in Time* and *Twenty Thousand Leagues under the Sea.*

# 3 Voyage and return

In this plot, the main character leaves to go to an unfamiliar country. Often, there is a door or gateway and the main character or characters are compelled to enter it. After facing increasingly difficult challenges, the protagonist returns home with stories to the disbelief of those around him. Stories written with this plot want the reader to be awed by the wonder of the new land. The emotional goals of the writer are to create in the reader a curiosity to go further. The author must fully explain *why* this new setting is important and intriguing. Examples include *Charlie and the*

*Chocolate Factory, Alice in Wonderland, The Wizard of Oz, The Lion, the Witch and the Wardrobe, Peter Pan, Gulliver's Travels.*

## 4 Comedy

In the context of traditional basic plots, a *comedy* means a romantic story with a happy ending. In the broadest definition, a comedy isn't necessarily full of jokes; it does not have a talking dog, nor is it full of catchphrases. In a comedy plot, the main characters are a couple seeking to develop their romantic relationship. The conflicts of the story are the obstacles that keep them apart. The author must fully explain *why* the couple needs a permanent commitment and how they get together in the end. Emotionally, the author tugs on the readers' heartstrings with romance, passion, sentiment and possibly humour. Examples include *A Midsummer Night's Dream, Much Ado about Nothing, Twelfth Night, Bridget Jones's Diary, The Notebook, Emma, The Windflower, Twilight* and *The Taming of the Shrew.*

## 5 Tragedy

A tragedy is a story of suffering. The main characters find themselves in worse and worse circumstances and make poorer and poorer choices and the story usually ends in death or destruction. The author must explain fully *why* the choices the main character makes are so destructive and *why* we as readers should care. Emotionally, the author is taking the reader through negative emotions such as sadness, hopelessness, confusion and despair. The death of the antagonist is often the perfect comeuppance. Examples include *Romeo and Juliet, Julius Caesar, The Hunchback of Notre Dame, Where the Red Fern Grows, Madame Bovary, Tuck Everlasting, Rebecca, The Outsiders, The Book Thief, Les Misérables* and *Anna Karenina.*

## 6 Rags to riches

This plot is usually the story of a humble main character who acquires wealth, power and connections. He then loses them, which only strengthens his inner virtues. The author must fully explain *why* the opportunities for the main character have arisen and why this changes their inner life. Often, rags-to-riches stories are used as life lessons or morality tales. A common theme in this plot is money doesn't buy happiness. Examples of this plot are *David Copperfield, Aladdin, The Magnificent Ambersons, Cinderella, Great Expectations* and *A Woman of Substance.*

## 7 Rebirth

This plot centres around an unlikeable main character whose circumstances or choices lead him to a moment of epiphany, repentance or redemption. The author must fully explain *why* these things change the main character. The author encourages the reader to hold out hope for him and cheer for the main character when he is successful. The emotional journey of the reader is a complicated one, moving from negative to more positive as the ending draws near. Examples are *Beauty and the Beast*, *A Christmas Carol*, *How the Grinch Stole Christmas*, *Crime and Punishment*, *The Scarlet Letter*, *The Catcher in the Rye* and *Strange Case of Dr Jekyll and Mr Hyde*.

## Workshop

Take Forster's example, 'The king died, and then the queen died of grief'.

- Choose a plot type, say *Tragedy*, and write for ten minutes on how that story could be told, touching on all the important whys and emotions of that plot.
- Then choose another plot, say, *Overcoming the monster*, and write on the same story for ten more minutes.

Compare the two story ideas. Make notes. Write something about what you learned and observed.

## Free write on plot

With the notes you've collected for your work in progress, choose the plot that's the best fit. Then free write for ten minutes about how your characters can meet the requirements of the plot. If you need help, start this way: *My quest story is about …*

Now, choose an entirely different plot and do the same thing, writing for ten minutes. Compare the two plots. What insight have you gained? What have you observed?

*The next chapter describes the requirements of the different genres of fiction and explains how you can create a convincing world within your novel that readers can believe in.*

# 7

## Genre and world building

Why do you need to know about different genres? You probably know the kind of story you want to write, but knowledge of genre will help you understand the rules for that kind of story. If you don't know yet what kind of story you want to write, then as you read about the different genres described in this chapter, you may be drawn to fantasy over romance or mysteries over science fiction.

No matter what genre you choose for your future story, you will have to create a world for it. Even if your imaginary world is outside your current reality, even if it is futuristic, interplanetary, or under the sea, the necessity for detail and smallness is still there. Your reader needs to believe that you *know* your world. The more intriguing and detailed you make your world, the more willing your readers will be to follow you there.

# Neil Gaiman

*'All fiction is a process of imagining: whatever you write, in whatever genre or medium, your task is to make things up convincingly and interestingly and new.'*

## The power of genre

In the 1954 Japanese film *The Seven Samurai,* a group of poor peasants hire a band of Samurai warriors to come and protect their village from a raid of marauding bandits. This film is considered a masterpiece and is often cited as one of the best ever made. The genre, of course, is *Japanese warrior* film, relying heavily on the setting to define it.

In 1960 American director John Sturgis made the film *The Magnificent Seven.* In this story, set in a Mexican village in the late 1800s, impoverished farmers request the help of local sharpshooters to protect them from a gang of thieves. *The Magnificent Seven* is the same story as *The Seven Samurai,* but the genre, *classic American Western,* is vastly different.

In 1998 Pixar Studios released their second children's animation film. *A Bug's Life* was the story of a group of anthropomorphic ants that is bullied by a group of local grasshoppers. An inventive ant named Flik discovers a gang of travelling circus bugs and coerces them into returning to his ant colony to protect them from their enemies. *A Bug's Life* has the same story as *The Seven Samurai* and *The Magnificent Seven* but the setting, the characters, the humour and the *telling* of the story safely put it in another genre altogether: *children's animation.* Children's animation films are full of slapstick, simple jokes and cute animals.

It's worth noting that this was Pixar's second film, but they probably had a vision even then of who they were as storytellers. Pixar had branded itself as a family film animation studio. Because of this, Pixar had rules to follow that the genre of family comedies dictated, so they removed the bawdiness of the original (and the English subtitles) and catered specifically to their intended audience.

This comparison of *The Seven Samurai, The Magnificent Seven* and *A Bug's Life* demonstrates the necessity and power of genre. Genre describes the categories of stories that follow specific rules attached to setting, tone or plot. Genre serves two purposes: to establish the rules so that readers know what to expect and to help brand the author in his marketing. Readers all over the world know that Zane Grey only writes *Westerns*, that Norah Ephron writes *romantic comedies*, that Jackie Collins writes *steamy romance* and that Stephen King writes *horror*. Most savvy authors never stray too far from the genre with which they are associated.

## Key idea

You can also take the familiar plots from other stories that you love and rewrite them into your preferred genre, as Pixar did.

## Robert McKee, *Story: Substance, Structure, Style, and the Principles of Screenwriting*

'[Genre is the] specific settings, roles, events, and values that define individual genres and their sub genres.'

It is in these four story elements that predictability is created for your reader. As you develop your story, you will need to make choices about the settings, roles, events and values of your book, not just for yourself and your own writing direction, but also for your future readers.

## Focus point

To add to the definition of story from the last section, now you're not only answering the question 'What is your story about, and why do those things happen?' but you're also answering the 'where' and 'when' and 'who'— answers that are almost always clarified in the genre. Remember, the classifications of genre are not always hard and fast.

# The genres of fiction

Below is a list of the most contemporary genres in Western literature. They generally represent *commercial fiction*. Commercial fiction, often called *genre fiction,* describes specifically categorized books that have plot-driven stories that could, conceivably, be experienced by the average reader. These stories have an emphasis on entertainment.

## MYSTERY

In the mystery genre, a crime has been committed early in first act and the remainder of the book is dedicated to identifying the persons responsible and their motives. The rules are:

- the protagonist is the key puzzle solver
- all the clues are revealed to the reader (even though they may not be recognized as clues)
- the solution is feasible.

Within this genre are subcategories that include amateur detective, forensic, medical, classic whodunnit, police procedural, comic, courtroom drama, private detective, cosy mystery, heists and capers, locked room, psychological suspense, romantic, and private investigator. Mysteries can be set in any time period.

## THRILLER

Stories that qualify as thrillers often begin with an impending threat to a large institution – for instance, *the citizens of Seattle will be murdered from poison in the drinking water*. The remainder of the book describes the action taken by the protagonist to thwart the threat and save the day. The rules are:

- the protagonist faces one white-knuckle escapade after another
- in the last climactic scene, he alone can face the villain who's behind it all.

Most thrillers are contemporary, but historical thrillers are not out of the question. The rules that define a thriller are more about plot than anything else. Within this genre are also subcategories such as historical, horror, political, eco-thriller, medical, legal, erotic, comic, military, romantic, action, crime, psychological, conspiracy, forensic, disaster, supernatural, police procedural, technological and espionage.

## ROMANCE

The best-selling genre of books worldwide, a romance generally has one objective: to get the couple that meets at the beginning of the story into a committed relationship. The rules are:

- the relationship is the central plot point
- the obstacles centre around keeping them from being together
- there is a happy-ever-after ending.

The point-of-view character is almost always one member of the couple. Within this genre are a multitude of subgenres that range from romantic comedies to historical romance in nearly any time period, to contemporary romance, erotica and homosexual romance. Romance is often found as subplots in other genres.

## WOMEN'S FICTION

Women's fiction is a broad category that describes stories about women's issues. The rules are:

- the story is written from a woman's point of view (usually in the first person)
- it's not necessarily centred around a romantic relationship
- it usually takes place during contemporary times.

Often the themes include career, family, divorce, children, infertility, self-sufficiency and independence. All chick-lit books fall into this genre; they are usually contemporary and use first-person point of view.

## HISTORICAL FICTION

This is a broad category that includes stories set outside contemporary settings. The rules are:

- the story is often centred around a specific historical event such as the sinking of the *Titanic*
- it requires vast amounts of research
- consistency is a must: readers of historical fiction won't tolerate laziness in their authors.

The rules are also dictated by the specific setting. Subgenres include Edwardian, Victorian, Regency, Elizabethan, Colonial, Amish or Puritan stories. Speculative historical fiction blurs the line between history and fantasy and could almost be considered a genre in its own right. Historical romance fuses two genres together.

## HORROR

Horror stories are identified by their emphasis on graphic violence, larger-than-life villains and possibly supernatural elements. The rules are:

- the tone is fearful and full of suspense
- the plot is fantastic with many unexpected events
- the reader feels increasing terror.

Horror stories can include the same elements as thrillers and mysteries. 'Overcoming the monster' is a frequent plot in horror stories and it is depicted as a battle between good and evil. Subgenres could include historical, child in peril, erotic, vampire, dark fantasy, gothic, fabulist, dark mystery, comic, hauntings, paranormal, creepy kids, magical realism, splatter, psychological and zombie.

## FANTASY

The fantasy genre is a broad one, and its most important feature is an element, somewhere, of magic, otherworldliness, paranormal events or characters, and *it cannot be real*. Fantasy often creates its own settings or entire worlds. The rules are:

- the author maintains consistency in the world he has created
- the story convinces the reader that this world and the author's purposes are important and intriguing enough to finish the book.

Nearly every plot will work within the fantasy genre. Subgenres of fantasy include dystopian, New Age, alternative history, post-apocalyptic, erotic, space opera, magical realism, sword and sorcery, game-related, biopunk, heroic, time travel, mythic fantasy, urban fantasy, historical, comic, vampire, Arthurian, zombie, cyberpunk, Bangsian, dark fantasy and alternative world.

## SCIENCE FICTION

Science-fiction novels are set against a technological or scientific backdrop, such as a spaceship or futuristic world; they could *potentially* be real. The rules are based on the restrictions of the setting. They are:

- the author has to convince the reader that the setting is complete and authentic
- the science and technology must be feasible.

The plots of the science-fiction genre are often quests, overcoming the monster or voyage and return, and because of that the characters are generally less developed. Science-fiction stories are more often plot driven than character driven. The author must also show that the mission of the characters is important and worth reading about. Subgenres include steampunk, cyberpunk, post-apocalyptic, time travel, near future, humorous and military.

## YOUNG ADULT

Young Adult fiction usually deals with the problems and concerns of contemporary young people. The rules are:

- the story is character driven and often written in the first person
- the main characters are between 17 and 25
- romance is touched on but it doesn't have to be the central plot of the story
- there is no graphic sex.

Young Adult fiction is generally rich in inner character development. A good example of literary young adult fiction is *The Fault in Our Stars*.

## NEW ADULT

New Adult fiction is similar to the Young Adult genre but the main characters are slightly older. The rules are:

- stories are character driven and often written in the first person
- characters are usually high-school or college graduates or 20-somethings who have just entered the professional world
- sex references may be more frequent in the story.

Plots involve contemporary issues and possibly romance, self-identity, coming of age and an emotional journey.

## CHRISTIAN

This is an extremely broad category of books encompassing all the other genres. The rules are:

- plots are centred around faith and the Judeo-Christian worldview
- there is a sense of justice, an optimistic ending and romantic love leads to marriage
- there is no graphic sex at all.

Dozens of agents and publishers specialize only in fiction that is consistent with Christian values.

# Focus point: literary fiction

Often called mainstream fiction, literary fiction comprises books that are hard to categorize. They have more character-driven stories that frequently answer life's big questions. The characters in literary fiction have a rich inner life. Literary fiction is sometimes creative and these stories are sometimes outside the experience of the average reader. They also place a strong emphasis on artistic language. Even if your preferred choice is literary, it is useful to know the rules of fiction in other genres.

# Genre and marketing

The problem with genre is that the categories are not fixed. Plots often merge two or more genres: for example, space aliens in Elizabethan London fall in love and identify the killer. However, identifying your preferred genre helps you not only to know the rules to follow but also to market it to future readers and publishers.

Once your story is finished, regardless of the method of publishing you choose, you will be required to explain your book in the fewest words possible. By knowing the various kinds of genres and subgenres, you can explain your book more succinctly. Publishers list the books that they are interested in by genre and agents often specialize in specific types of genre. Bookshop owners have shelves devoted to specific genres. They'll want to know whether your fantasy should go with steampunk, Arthurian or erotica. Genres and subgenres are also useful as key words in Amazon searches – which are the tools that your potential readers could use to find you. Genres are immensely helpful for everyone associated with publishing: writers, agents, publishers and sellers.

# Focus point

At this point in your story sculpting, it's not critical that you choose a genre, but it will be eventually. Refer to the list of genres during the drafting process to make sure that you are following the rules for your preferred genre.

## Your preferred genre

Think about your favourite books and tally which ones are in which genre. Do you favour one genre over another or are your tastes varied? Why is this?

Return to the answer you gave in Chapter 1, the one about seeing yourself at a book signing. What genre was the book you wrote about?

## Workshop

- Have you already chosen a specific genre for your work in progress? If you have, ask yourself whether it follows the rules mentioned above. Then spend ten minutes answering this:

  'My work-in-progress fits this genre because …'

- If you don't yet have a genre for your work, review the notes you made in Chapter 4. Are there anecdotes, desires, ideas or patterns that lean toward a specific genre? Could they, with a little creativity and imagination?

- Now think about book covers. Often in genre fiction, the book cover itself says a lot about what to expect in the book. Spend ten minutes doodling, sketching or even looking at other book covers on the Internet that fit your chosen genre.

# World building

## Robert McKee, *Story: Substance, Structure, Style, and the Principles of Screenwriting*

*'An honest story is at home in one place and time.'*

The sculpting of your work in progress is now moving into more intimate detail. You started with a definition of story, then you moved on to plot and genre. Now you're moving into building a world, or what McKee calls in his definition of story 'consistent and causally connected fictional reality'. You will now start to think about building the detailed reality for your story.

Jane Austen created 'consistent and causally connected' worlds for her books. Rural England in the early nineteenth century had specific rules to follow. Her story was clearly similar to her reality, so she didn't have to reinvent weather or social customs, dress or language. But she did have to create small towns, social structures and reasons why certain things happened the way they did. For example, the legal issue of *entailment* was critical for the plot in *Pride and Prejudice*.

Austen presumably organized her world to create conflicts between men and women, higher and lower classes, young and old, within the social expectations of her real-life world. For all their passions, neither Emma nor Lizzie Bennet would have sought gainful employment; that would have broken societal rules. And Lady Catherine de Bourgh would never have grown literal fangs, because that would have broken physical ones. (Her figurative fangs were fun enough!) Austen made these choices for her setting, perhaps because she knew no better, and she remained consistent in them. As a result, readers found her stories believable and authentic, which meant that they were more than willing to travel on the emotional journey with the author, even though the settings Highbury and Meryton were fictional.

Austen's settings were small spaces: small towns, families and social structures in which she was comfortable. She wrote what she knew. Because of her intimate knowledge of this small area, she was able to plunge deeply into the detail of her little towns. Would Mrs Bates have been so annoying if *Emma* had taken place in London, where the social circles would have been broader? And if Emma's social circle was broader, she would have been far too busy to find herself a Harriet. (And poor Mr Woodhouse would have found the city disagreeable to his health.) Authors who choose intimate settings have the advantage of doing what Austen did: filling their settings with detail. The more detail and work an author puts into his setting, the more fully he understands it, the more original his story becomes and the less likely it is that he will be haunted by clichés.

## Robert McKee, *Story: Substance, Structure, Style, and the Principles of Screenwriting*

'The larger the world, the more diluted the knowledge of the writer, therefore the fewer his creative choices and the more clichéd the story. The smaller the world, then, the more complete the knowledge of the writer, therefore the greater his creative choices. Result: a fully original story and victory in the war on cliché!'

No matter what genre you choose for your future story, you will have to create a complete and detailed world for it, one that convinces your reader to believe in it. Only if your world is fully believable will your readers be able to immerse themselves in your story.

Creating this detailed, three-dimensional setting that includes places, time in history, time frame and societal and cultural norms takes a lot of work. The following workshop comprises several exercises and each one may take longer to do than ten minutes. In fact, the more time you put into them the better your story will be. There isn't any limit to world building. Do the following exercises as thoroughly as possible. Keep in mind, though, that like every other choice you are making, there will be time later to change your mind, alter things a bit or eliminate certain ideas. Nothing is set in stone.

## Workshop

Answer the following questions for the setting of your work in progress. The more detail you can add, the better. Save all of this, possibly in separate files for each point. And as you answer the questions, think about the smallest unit you can to allow you to develop more details.

### 1. Time

A. In what year does this story take place?

B. On what day of that year does it begin?

C. Over how much time will this story take place: days, weeks or months?

D. What cultural or social events will take place during that time frame, which you must acknowledge? For example, in *Emma*, Emma's social gatherings were structured around the calendar year, starting with a summer wedding. They included a Christmas party later and Austen wrapped up the story in the summer the following year. A limited time frame may be helpful in making your world more real.

E. What personal experiences can you add to this setting to enhance the details? If you need help, return to the notes you wrote in Chapter 4.

F. What conflicts might arise from the time frame you have chosen?

## 2. Place

A. In what city or town does your story take place?

B. In what specific part of that city or town?

C. What personal experiences can you add to this setting to enhance the details? For example, the house you have your hero living in could look just like your grandmother's.

D. What conflicts could arise from the location you have chosen?

E. What interiors and exteriors are necessary for the telling of the story? In *Emma*, Jane Austen included the Woodhouse home of Hartfield, Donwell Abbey, Box Hill, the village of Highbury, the local miller's shop, Mrs Bates's home, Mrs Goddard's school and a local spot where they held their dances.

F. What personal experiences can you add to this setting to enhance the details? If you need help, return to the notes you wrote in Chapter 4.

G. What conflicts could arise from the specific locations you have chosen?

H. What climate and geographic rules must you follow?

I. What conflicts could arise from the climate or geography?

### 3. Culture

A. What cultural or social rules must you follow?

B. What conflicts could arise from the culture or social norms?

C. What technological or scientific rules must you follow? In *Emma*, the story takes place in 1816, so all the technology had to be consistent with the time.

D. What conflicts could arise from the technology or science in the world you created?

E. What personal experiences can you add to this setting to enhance the details? If you need help, return to the notes you wrote in Chapter 4.

### 4. Your own experience

Return to any notes you've made in your daily observations about setting. Is there anything you can use?

## Where to next?

*The driver of your plot and the focus of your story is your main character, or protagonist. The next chapter explains the four main stages in developing your protagonist so that he or she is believable, authentic and worth reading about.*

# 8

# The protagonist

The fun part of sculpting a novel, arguably, is creating the character the story is about. In all novels, the main character (or protagonist) is the character around which all the central action takes place. The protagonist faces the most conflicts in the achievement of his or her ultimate goal, generates the most sympathy or interest from the reader and possesses the inner drives that dictate the course of the plot. If a protagonist is developed well, these drives will be mutually exclusive, they will cumulate into a difficult choice, and the emotional, satisfying ending will fascinate the reader.

This chapter will help you thoroughly develop your main character. For the sake of thoroughness, and on the assumption that your ideas for main characters are not complete, we are going to go through the four stages of developing a character from scratch: archetype, basic description, characterization and desires.

Suzanne Collins, *The Hunger Games*

*'I am not pretty. I am not beautiful. I am as radiant as the sun.'*

Katniss Everdeen, 16 years old, sole breadwinner of a single-parent family in a futuristic, post-apocalyptic dystopian society, is one of the most complex and intriguing characters in modern literature. She is, indeed, as radiant as the sun, blazing and glorious and forever fixed in the minds of the readers as the cunning, valiant and vulnerable hero of *The Hunger Games*.

Author Suzanne Collins gave Katniss specific character traits, tastes and skills and tapped into her complex past to make this heroine believable and authentic. What makes *The Hunger Games* such a great story is not just the rich world Collins created or the high-concept plot, but Katniss's conflicting drives and desires as the tension increases (and there is a *lot* of tension in *The Hunger Games*). Her battles become the readers' battles. Arguably, few readers can get to the end of the book without weeping or being moved by Katniss's words and actions and their consequences. This is what made the book so successful: the multifaceted, dynamic main character.

Readers winced when Katniss was injured, hoped she would find favour, wept when she faced indescribable loss, trembled as she faced her fears and celebrated as she claimed her victories. Like Katniss, the readers of *The Hunger Games* have had to fight for justice, they've had to lay their lives down for others, they know what it's like to choose suffering so that someone else can be safe. The readers identify with Katniss Everdeen. The readers are, despite living in relative comfort and not fighting someone to the death, *like* her. They want solutions. They want justice. They want safety. They want victory. When readers *love* a story, often it's because they identify so strongly with the characters.

There are as many ways to create a well-defined character as there are novels for sale in a well-stocked charity shop. Some authors develop characters based on favourites from other stories. Some find inspiration from a relationship. Some create a backstory from the creepy lady they saw at the station who looked just like Michael Jackson. Other authors have to start with nothing. You will have to create your characters, too, and make them living, breathing and worth reading about.

Conveniently, the four stages of developing character flow nicely in alphabetical order:

1  **Archetype:** The archetype is only a template. Archetypes are broad categories of character, originally used in the theatre of ancient Greece and a familiar model in traditional Western stories that your reader will recognize. An archetype is not meant to be specific, but assigning an archetype to your character gives you a general framework to build upon. This is similar to choosing a plot or a genre. These general choices provide familiarity and allow your reader to trust you as the story progresses.

2  **Basic description:** Basic description is the basic information about your main character. This includes everything someone would notice about the character if they saw them walking down the street: their appearance, age, clothing, gait, posture, etc.

3  **Characterization:** Characterization is the personality and preferences of a character. This is the information you would find out on a Facebook page or a dating profile. This can include religion, music choices, education, work history, demeanour and quirks. This can also include information that is not public, such as secrets, weaknesses and fears.

4  **Desires:** Desires are the most intimate parts of a character; *what he wants more than anything in the world*. This character may not even be *aware* of what desires he has. He may *say* he wants something but, in reality, he wants something else. All the other facets of character development can be varied and imaginative, but human desires are common to everyone. Because of this, it is in the *desires* that the reader can identify with the character the most. Desires like security, love, acceptance and freedom are universal. The best stories in the world are all about conflicting desires, like those of Katniss Everdeen who risks her family's survival for freedom.

# Archetype

The first step in developing character is choosing an archetype. An archetype is a prototype of character in fiction that is predictable. Archetypes are a template, so to speak, of the character that is to come and are not meant to be complete. By choosing an archetype, an author makes broad, decisive strokes; the finer details of the character will be worked out through the basic description, characterization and desires. Lazy writers stop at this phase, creating flat, predictable, dull characters. Thorough writers keep going.

Author Tami Cowden, in her book *The Complete Guide to Heroes and Archetypes,* lists 16 different archetype forms: eight for male and eight for female protagonists. These archetypes are, she explains, the most common types of protagonists in fiction. By choosing a template-like archetype in the beginning, the author then can expand upon it and make something unique and intriguing.

## ARCHETYPES OF MALE PROTAGONISTS

These are Cowden's archetypes for male protagonists with examples from literature, film and television. The examples listed may not be a perfect fit for the archetype. But that's the point. A good writer uses the archetype as a foundation and then creates the details, the characterization and the desires of the character to make it unique.

### The chief

This character is instantly recognizable as the commander, the one who makes quick, good decisions. This character is fearless, easily respected, usually an alpha male, and more goal-oriented than people-oriented. Positive chiefs have inspirational vision, are charismatic and can utilize the resources around them. The negative chiefs lean toward being a bully or a braggart, who may be leading with ulterior motives or to stroke his own ego. Chiefs are often the 'white hat cowboy' who saves the town, or the CEO or starship captain who outmanoeuveres the aliens. The chief can have myriad desires, but usually love and acceptance are not nearly as important as survival or the greater good. Examples include Michael Corleone, Captain Kirk, Indiana Jones, Charles Foster Kane, Jack Aubrey, Aragorn and Fitzwilliam Darcy.

### The bad boy

The bad boy is the often-quiet brooder who thinks before he speaks. He has a rap sheet, a chip on his shoulder and distaste for authority. This character is rebellious, a bit mysterious and doesn't follow anyone. He actually prefers to be alone. Unlike our chief, the street-smart bad boy leads others for mostly selfish reasons. Bad boys are often anti-heroes or the leather-jacketed bikers who don't mind being misunderstood. It may have been the bad boy who invented the *smoulder*. The bad boy's biggest drive may be basic – survival – but it could also be something hidden like a father's acceptance or the need for family. Examples include Hawkeye Pierce, George Costanza, Bugs Bunny, Rick Blaine from *Casablanca*, James Dean and J.J. Gittes from *Chinatown*.

## The best friend

The best friend is often portrayed as a benign nice guy who avoids confrontation and is far more people-oriented than goal-oriented. The best friend could be the guy who has a crush on one girl for years. He could be puppy-like: faithful, cute and adorable at times. He could also be self-sacrificial, forfeiting his own happiness for the dream girl's or his family's or for duty or honour. Generally, best friends are beta males, often portrayed as nerdy or clumsy and so, when they do get the girl, their triumph is all the more glorious. They are often the classic underdog and readers *love* them. They can have a variety of desires, but security or acceptance is often one of the most important ones. Examples include Charles Bingley, Chandler Bing, Woody Allen in nearly all his movies, Samwise Gamgee, Mickey Mouse, George Michael Bluth, Kermit the Frog, George Bailey and Snoopy.

## The charmer

Usually good-looking and charismatic, the charmer is a guy who is full of himself and his stories. He enters like a tornado and gains attention through his larger-than-life persona. The charmer is the guy who dates the girl whom the 'best friend' is in love with, which could mean that he's really cheating on her or using her for his narcissistic self-narrative. The charmer is seductive and exciting; he is impulsive and adventurous; he's often involved in organized crime. He is also irresponsible, unreliable and often a liar. He frequently uses his charm and personality to get himself out of trouble, and is shocked if this tactic doesn't work. Charmers may also be vain and obsessed with appearances. The charmer appears to be driven by wanting to have a good time, but if you dig deeper, you may find an insecure boy wanting acceptance from others. Examples include Rhett Butler, Merry and Pippin from *The Lord of the Rings*, Mr Elton, Don Lockwood, Cosmo Kramer, Peter Pan and Jay Gatsby.

## The lost soul

The lost soul is like a bad boy without the criminal record. The lost soul is a thoughtful, pensive, over-thinking poet or artist, even though his day job may be something altogether different. The lost soul is secretive and rarely shares his thoughts with others. The positive lost souls are those hidden geniuses, while the negative ones are the ones who may be obsessed with a specific girl and then get arrested for stalking – or worse. The deep thoughts of a lost soul are what make them attractive to the opposite sex, but they are rarely the alpha male, the fighter or the commander. The lost soul is also more often anti-hero than hero and his conflicts are far more internal than external. The biggest driver of the lost soul is an ideal world or to be accepted by peers or family. Examples include the Phantom in *Phantom of the Opera*, Hamlet, Don Draper, Don Quixote, Frodo Baggins, Boo Radley, Willy Loman and Charlie Brown.

## The professor

The professor may be easy to spot. He has taped glasses, a tweed jacket and books under his arm. He's absorbed with his theories or his thesis or his dissertation and he has little time for others. But his brain is also his greatest asset. He'll be the one who fixes the formula for the antidote that saves the world from bioterrorism. He'll know the obscure trivia that solves the case. He is the one whom others turn to when they're stumped. He is also a faithful friend, not terribly romantic, but steady, nonetheless, to people around him. At best, he's a hero like Mr Spock or Sherlock Holmes, or even a Tony Stark, and at worst he slips into sociopathic tirades with his criminal mastermind. He can be a bit obsessive and legalistic and compartmentalizes everything, but he knows his stuff. The professor's biggest drive could be acceptance of his intelligence or it could be the greater good. But the professor might have to be reminded that true love, friendship and family are important. Examples include Ross Geller from *Friends*, Atticus Finch, Mr Collins, Ashley Wilkes, Perry Mason, Gandalf, Mr Spock, Sherlock Holmes and Linus van Pelt.

## The swashbuckler

This guy is like the charmer, but not afraid to get dirty. His modus operandi is all about the stunt, the physical fight, the drama of fast action. The swashbuckler is seen in all the old Errol Flynn movies of the early twentieth century and he can be seen today whenever a hero shows that he can take down an assassin with a rolled-up magazine, like Jason Bourne. He is respected less for his inner character and brains than his skill set – which could include martial arts, fencing, acrobatics or anything else athletic or physical. Where the chief would make a plan and follow through, the swashbuckler kicks, punches, attacks, leaps or charges first and asks questions later. The swashbuckler is heroic and so his drives are often for survival, safety and accomplishment. Examples include Tom Sawyer, Huckleberry Finn, Captain Jack Sparrow, Legolas and Gimli, Captain Malcolm Reynolds, James Bond and Tintin.

## The warrior

The warrior is the physical hero who fights for a cause or for someone weaker. His motivating drive is justice or virtue. Like the swashbuckler, he fights and uses his physical skills to hinder the bad guy, but the warrior has a specific mission: to protect others. He's more noble and altruistic than the swashbuckler. He's a superhero. The warrior is not afraid to break convention or rebel against authority to meet his goals. He is driven, fearless and virtuous. The warrior is not usually a deep thinker or overly emotional. His drives are basic: survival, the greater good and high ideals. Examples include Superman, Robin Hood, Batman, Spiderman, Steve Rogers (*Captain America*), Thor, Jake Lamotta, King Arthur and GI Joe.

## ARCHETYPES OF FEMALE PROTAGONISTS

Much has been written lately about the need for strong female leads in modern literature. Each of the following archetypes has a specific type of strength; they can all defend themselves in unpredictable ways and a writer can sculpt them in such a way that readers can admire them. If readers think that female protagonists should be able to excel in martial arts in order to be defined as strong, then it is because authors haven't skilfully created female heroines and put them in intriguing stories.

## The boss

An easy archetype to recognize, the boss is a woman who commands respect, whether she deserves it or not. Often bumping her head on the glass ceiling, she is ambitious, driven and authoritative, pursuing achievement at the expense of relationships. She sees herself as empowered and indestructible and wants to prove to the world that she's capable and strong. A positive boss is an Eleanor Roosevelt or a Condoleeza Rice. A negative boss would ignore her family, backstab her co-workers and alienate her superiors. The boss is easily identified in the boardroom, but is just as recognizable in a police force or in school administration. Her basic drive is money, position or accomplishment. Examples include Lady Catherine de Burgh, Lady Macbeth, Leslie Knope, Miss Piggy, Lucy van Pelt, Ripley from *Alien* and Mrs Bennet.

## The survivor

The survivor is much like the boss, but it's less about personal accomplishment and more about living to see the next day. Survivors are less scrupulous and less likely to be leaders; they are driven by their cynicism and fear and want to prevent disaster. The survivor has a broad arsenal of tricks up her sleeve: she's charming, often beautiful. She uses her cunning, her sex appeal and her education to get what she wants. The survivor sees more than she lets on and uses others' weaknesses to her advantage. The survivor is a Scarlett O'Hara, who thinks nothing of exploiting her family and friends for the sake of security. Security is a survivor's biggest drive and, if you get in her way, you can bet she'll cut you. Examples include Katniss Everdeen, Eowyn from *The Lord of the Rings*, Princess Leia, Lily Bart, Holly Golightly, Lara Croft, Rosie the Riveter and Scarlett O'Hara.

## The spunky kid

The spunky kid is not particularly ambitious but she sure is fun to be around. The spunky kid is usually cute, optimistic and well liked. She is supportive and a hard worker. She's great to have on a team and play the best friend or the girl-next-door. The spunky kid surprises herself with the way she stands up to a bully or solves a problem. She may lean toward the romantic and ideal, not the seductive. She usually lacks cynicism and negativity. She often has a big heart and is the source of many 'Aww' moments. She may be the girl that draws a smiley on the 'i' in her name, lives next door to you and wants to change the world. Her biggest drives are ideals and virtues and the greater good. She may even neglect her own needs for the sake of others. Examples include Pippi Longstocking, Eliza Doolittle, Laura from *Little House on the Prairie*, Nancy Drew, Kathy Selden from *Singin' in the Rain*, Mary Richards and Mary Ann from *Gilligan's Island*.

## The free spirit

Like the spunky kid, the free spirit is fun to be around, but she is more imaginative, more poetic and more idealistic. The free spirit usually has a unique fashion sense, is experimental in her philosophies and relationships, and impulsive to the point of it being a weakness. She is often artistic and trendsetting. She is often oblivious and, at her worst, a bit narcissistic. Do not go to the free spirit for practical help or advice, or put her in a place where she has to use her skills or her wits to survive. She may be too dependent on others, too ditzy or too emotional to be much good. She will throw great parties, however, and have great stories to tell. Her biggest drives are immediate – perhaps fame or opportunity – or a great new pair of shoes. She's not particularly altruistic or heroic, and if she winds up saving the day, it's mostly because she wasn't paying attention and it kind of fell into her lap. Examples include Emma Woodhouse, Anne Shirley, Beatrice from *Much Ado about Nothing*, Blanche DuBois, Juliet Capulet, Disney's Merida and Phoebe from *Friends*.

## The waif

The waif is an easily recognizable female archetype. She's particularly helpless and childlike, unless you uncover her wilfulness. The waif can hide her strengths easily. Under her damsel-in-distress persona, she may be stronger or smarter than she lets on. Her childlikeness may put her perpetually in a role of victim. Her empathetic tendencies and head-in-the-clouds idealism may get her into trouble. She often has a past full of suffering and hardship and is looking for a rescue or a rescuer. Old-fashioned fairy tales often put the waif in their lead roles, like *Sleeping Beauty* or *Cinderella* or *Rapunzel*. Lucy Pevensie in *The Chronicles of Narnia* is a great example of a waif; she is the most innocent and trusting of her siblings and, despite her weakness, she has the closest relationship with Aslan. Examples include Scout Finch in *To Kill a Mockingbird*, Sara Crewe in *A Little Princess*, Ophelia from *Hamlet*, Dorothy Gale from *The Wizard of Oz* and Cosette from *Les Misérables*.

## The librarian

The librarian has an instant visual: the studious woman with a bun and thick glasses. This woman values education and knowledge more than relationships and passion. At her worst, she's cold, isolating herself from the world. At her best, she embraces her inner passions and uses her beauty as well as her brain for her own happiness. She is practical and proper, the class nerd, a teacher's pet, who compensates for her lack of social skills with a sharp wit, a know-it-all attitude or a bit of condescension. She could be shy or bossy, lonely or admired, a hidden beauty or a Plain Jane, but her driving motivation is self-education and perhaps educating others. In a crisis, she will be practical and calculating. Examples include Jo in *Little Women*, Elizabeth in *Pride and Prejudice*, Miss Marple, Meg Murry from *A Wrinkle in Time*, Hermione Granger from the Harry Potter series, Harriet the Spy and Marian the Librarian from *The Music Man*.

## The crusader

The crusader could be a female superhero or warrior who seeks justice, vengeance or the common good. She could also have a cause: modern crusaders may lobby classroom parties for sugar-/ dairy-/gluten-free items and their great-grandmothers would have promoted Prohibition. The crusader, at her best, is Wonder Woman who gets the bad guy. At her worst, she believes that everyone should embrace her cause regardless. She is determined and stubborn and she has an arsenal of weapons – either an invisible jet, the ability to fly or her Congressman's number on speed dial. She gets riled up easily, especially when her children are involved. You do not want to go against her. Her drives are her pet causes and they are often a part of something bigger like a social problem, an injustice or public safety. Examples include Lisbeth Salandar in *The Girl with the Dragon Tattoo*, Buffy the Vampire Slayer, Norma Rae, Erin Brockovich, Karen Silkwood and Elastigirl from *The Incredibles*.

## The nurturer

The nurturer's strongest assets are her arms: she's always cuddling, consoling or carrying something for someone else. The nurturer listens well, keeps the peace, organizes her environment and places high value on the physical and emotional well-being of the people around her. She is strong in a quiet way, cheerful and full of hope. She is the idealistic Madonna, the June Cleaver, Melanie Wilkes, Mary Bailey type of woman who harks back to traditional stories. She appears weak because she's usually calm and quiet, but she is far from it. Her friends and family would fall apart without her. And it is her faith and hope that usually steer them out of trouble. She uses her gentleness and calmness to soothe the savage beasts around her and as a result, she is loved and respected universally. Wendy in *Peter Pan* is a nurturer and so are Mary Poppins, Maria von Trapp, Mrs Miniver and Leigh Anne Tuohy from *The Blind Side*.

## Looking at archetypes

1 Once you have read through the archetypes given in this chapter, try to come up with examples of your own. If you disagree with the ones listed, analyse why.

2 Then select three common literary archetypes that you love, both male and female. Give specific examples of each and describe why you love them.

3 Go through your personal library and try to categorize as many main characters into archetypes as you can. Explain how they meet the requirements of the archetype. Notice that you may discover main characters that don't fit into any archetype perfectly – it may be that they are developed so well and uniquely that they can't be pigeonholed.

## Workshop

For ten minutes, consider the archetype that best fits your main character. Write about why this would be a good fit, what their motivations would be and any other insight you have. Remember that this is an archetype, a loose blueprint or template of a character. There are still three more steps in the character-building process to make your character full and rich and worth reading about.

- If you are confident in the formation of your characters already, then free write about what you have already done, hitting all the major points of that archetype's requirements and then brainstorm about any additional information you need for the development of your character.
- If you haven't the first idea about what your main character should be, then do a ten-minute free write on each archetype. You may gain fresh insight into the basic form your character should take.

# Basic description

If you stop your protagonist's character development at the archetype stage, it would be like telling a story with paper dolls. Because your readers, unfortunately, are too familiar with archetypes, they could at this point, without interference from you, tell the story themselves. To make your story full of surprises and entice your reader, you need to build on the archetypes' predictability.

Use this framework and add a basic descripton. Your character needs a face, a background, a sense of humour – your character needs a soul. What is it then that you can add to your main character to flesh it out, to put muscles and bones on this skeleton?

*Hunger Games* author Suzanne Collins gives her reader Katniss's description this way: 'I watch as Gale pulls out his knife and slices the bread. He could be my brother. Straight black hair, olive skin, we even have the same gray eyes. But we're not related, at least not closely.'

Katniss's appearance is simply described. Her dark appearance is easy for the reader to mentally picture. Suzanne Collins didn't describe noses, height or specific clothing. Those details were not necessary for the reader to know, but Suzanne Collins knew what they were. In a few more sentences, Collins gives the reader even more insight as to who Katniss is: 'I stole eggs from nests, caught fish in nets, sometimes managed to shoot a squirrel or rabbit for stew, and gathered the various plants that sprung up beneath my feet … I kept us alive.'

The readers can picture her in their minds. They can see her as skilled, quiet, lonely and probably disturbed.

## Building your character

Answer the following questions about your main character only. For the sake of simplicity, these exercises will use the pronoun *he*.

1 What is his name? General convention says choose something that is not too hard to pronounce, no invented spellings and something that fits your setting. (Katniss would never be named Mackenzie or Ashleigh.)

2 What is his place and date of birth? Consider his birth order, which also plays a role. Consider how his siblings shape his personality.

3 What was the economic station of your main character's family?

4 What does your main character look like? How tall is he? What is his hair colour and style and what colour are his eyes? What are his height and weight, skin tone, body type and distinguishing characteristics? How does he walk, dress and groom himself?

5 Is your main character academically smart? Street smart? Imaginative? Socially savvy? Describe how he uses his intelligence to meet his goals. What skills does he have?

6 What is his education? His talents? His hobbies? Is he healthy? Does he have any bad habits?

7 In any of your previous notes, have you observed something in someone else that you could use for this character – the way they walked, a specific outfit or a catchphrase?

# Characterization

You know your character because of the archetype choice you made. You know what he looks like and perhaps some of his background. But *who is he?* What is the deeper, choice-making part of the person you are writing about?

The true nature of your character is his characterization. When we think of the people we are closest to, we don't immediately think of their appearance or their name. We may think of how impatient they are with the pizza delivery boy. How they cut corners when they are asked to do simple tasks. How they have a tendency to tear up at sad movies. How they are sympathetic towards those who are hurting. We think of their unique traits, positive and negative, their habits and preferences, their personalities. Unlike the people around you, though, your characters can be extremes: they can laugh more loudly, be more inventive, more successful, wittier, more annoying and more frustrating than the average person. You are free to exaggerate and expand your main character in any way you want.

As you sculpt your protagonist into the character you want him to be, don't make choices for the sake of making choices. Sculpt their characterization in such a way as to help or hinder the objective at hand. For example, Katniss Everdeen was already skilled as a hunter and tracker long before she stepped into the ring of the Hunger Games. This made the story better, enhanced her conflicts and kept the reader interested in how she would use her skills to survive. If she had been a flighty homebody or a delicate flower, she wouldn't have lasted ten seconds at the Cornucopia. She was a complicated character and her development was a rich one. Her past was spelled out – she had lost her father and had to support her mother based on the problems in her dystopian setting. This *shaped her* and it was this key part of her past that made her into the survivor that she was. It wasn't just her skill set, but her past, her analytical mind, her sense of observation and her quick reflexes that kept the readers' interest and the story moving.

 Robert McKee, *Story: Substance, Structure, Style, and the Principles of Screenwriting*

'The function of character is to bring to the story the qualities of characterization necessary to convincingly act out choices. Put simply, a character must be credible: young enough or old enough, strong or weak, worldly or naive, educated or ignorant, generous or selfish, witty or dull, in the right proportions. Each must bring to the story the combination of qualities that allows an audience to believe that the character could and would do what he does.'

## THE FOUR CORNERSTONES OF CHARACTER

How do we develop our character in progress into someone who is believable and living? How do we sculpt them into the perfect character for the plot we're putting them into?

M.J. Bush, writing coach and fantasy writer, uses what she calls the 'four cornerstones': The Fear, the Secret, the Flaw and the Quirk. By formulating these four traits in the character, much of our main character's fullness can be discovered. These four cornerstones are evident in Katniss's life in *The Hunger Games*:

- Her biggest fear is that her little sister won't be cared for.
- Her biggest secret is how she feels about the young men in her life.
- Her biggest flaw is her inability to trust.
- Her biggest quirk is her mockingjay pin.

## Discovering your character's traits

Spend ten minutes sculpting the four cornerstones of your character in progress.

1 What is your character really afraid of?

2 What is your character hiding?

3 What is your character's biggest weakness?

4 What is odd or unusual about your character?

## Workshop

Answer each of the following questions for your main character, but choose thoughtfully. Consider how the characteristic chosen can add conflict or help the character achieve his ultimate goal. Feel free to return to any notes from previous exercises for further insight. (If you find this workshop redundant in fleshing out your character, skip it.)

1 Is your character flighty or dependable?

2 Is your character warm and open or cold and hard to know?

3 Does your character exhibit fairness or does he cheat?

4 Is he smart or is he below average intellectually?

5 Is he culturally aware or ignorant of the world around him?

6 Is he conscious of others or oblivious to others?

7 Does he trust his friends and family or does he suspect they will hurt him?

8 Does he work hard at all he does or is he lazy and does he cut corners?

9 Is he secure in who he is or self-conscious?

10 Does he relax easily or is he uptight?

11 Are his emotions on an even keel or does he fly off the handle?

12 Does he have a lot of energy for physical and emotional challenges or does he weaken easily?

13 Does he pick up non-verbal cues well or is his only perception what people say?

14 Does he anger easily? If so, about what? Or is he patient and kind with others?

15 Is he a problem solver and practical or does he value more impractical things?

16 Does he want to learn more about life or is he not particularly curious?

17 Is he sociable and willing to talk to and meet others or does he prefer solitude?

18 Is he creative? Does he see things others don't? Or is he confined to his own traditions and rules?

19 Is he well organized and orderly in his surroundings or thoughtless and cluttered?

20 Does he find people energizing or does he find time alone more energizing?

## Describe your main character

Review all your notes on character up to this point, including the archetype, basic description and characterization and then, for ten minutes, do a free write describing your main character. Write as if he were a real person or even a family member. Get as much written as you can. Note what you focused on and what you omitted. What insight did you receive in this writing?

## Make your character fit your story

Return to your notes on plot, genre and setting. Free write for ten minutes on how the choices you made for plot and genre can work for or against your choices for your main character. Do you see any inconsistencies? Reshape your character as much as you think you need to to fit your story. Return to previous exercises and change whatever answers you need to.

### Key idea

It is worth seeking out other personality or character resources such as the Meyers Briggs Type Indicator or Four Temperaments Theory for additional insight into human personalities and tendencies. Novelists often use these tools to help them understand human nature better.

## Desires

You probably picked up this book because your dreams have become lost in a list of have-tos. You have your own conflict. You want to be responsible and care for others around you, yet you want to find time to pursue your own dreams. You are driven by your desires, as you should be.

Fortunately for you, your many desires are not mutually exclusive. But all your character's desires must be, for the sake of story. What *does* your main character want more than anything else in the world? And *why* does your main character do what he does? The answer may lie in a theory of human behaviour.

In 1943 psychologist Abraham Maslow asked the question, 'Why do people do what they do?' From that he created his famous hierarchy of needs to explain the basic motivations of the human race. Typically, this theory, which was later illustrated by a triangle shape (Figure 8.1), is used in behavioural psychology, education and in other fields associated with the human mind. And what can be said for the human race most certainly holds true for fictional characters.

## Victoria Mixon, *The Art and Craft of Fiction*

*'All fiction hinges on authenticity – the details of your characters' world, the way they speak, the way they move, the logic of how their mistakes blow up into ever-bigger and bigger mistakes until their lives come crashing down upon their heads.'*

Because your ultimate goal is authenticity – that you succeed in creating such a world, such a plot and such a character that your reader can't help but be drawn into it – you must give your characters an authentic human struggle. Maslow's hierarchy is potentially another tool in your character-sculpting bag. You must know, *really* know, why your character does what he does. What does he want, more than anything else?

## Focus point

Our study of plot notwithstanding, all stories come to this: someone wants something and he can't have it.

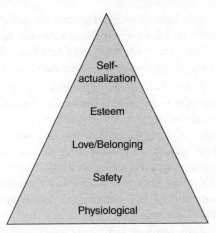

Figure 8.1: Maslow's hierarchy of needs

Maslow's theory presumes that everyone has the same needs and that they increase in complexity. The most important and basic needs for humans are at the bottom of the triangle. The needs then build upon each other, theoretically implying that one can't move to the next level of needs until the previous level is met, although it's been argued that someone (fictional or not) can pursue more than one simultaneously.

When we pick our character's deepest desires, we are choosing the root of who they are. The archetype, the basic description and the characterization are still only foggy impressions. It is our desires – our deepest human drives – that define us. In *The Hunger Games,* Katniss's drives are there because she has been raised in a brutal environment where few have their basic needs met. So her daily need for food, clothing and shelter is ingrained in her. This drive forms her skills, forms her thoughts and forms what she does every single day – legally or not – to meet these needs. If you want to analyse Katniss's drives, you could, and then you would see why this makes her such a rich character. Katniss is fighting on every page for her basic survival.

The most basic needs, the bottom of the triangle, are **physiological**. These include what every living creature needs – the need to breathe, eat, drink, procreate, sleep and excrete. Major characters whose main desires are in this level want this: protection from the elements, the next meal, a way to escape a literal monster, water to quench their thirst, and a place to rest through the night. Other examples of this in literature are *Oliver Twist, The Old Man and the Sea, Hatchet, Lord of the Flies, Life of Pi, Island of the Blue Dolphins, My Side of the Mountain, The Book Thief, The Odyssey, The Grapes of Wrath, Gone with the Wind, Watership Down* and *Moby Dick*.

The next level of needs is for **safety**. This includes basic security, adequate resources, a moral code, a family unity, gainful employment, good health and personal property. A need in this level is more than just having a roof over your head; it's having a permanent roof of a sturdy house. It's more than just having enough calories to function; it's having enough food for the winter. It's more than just guarding your family from assault; it's knowing that the laws of the land will help keep you safe. It's not about a sex life; it's about monogamy. Characters in this life stay in bad jobs for the sake of a paycheque, compromise morality for the sake of safety, and never dream of 'finding themselves'. The biggest conflicts in this level come from characters that don't feel secure or safe in the physical sense. Characters whose desires are in this level want to control their future, want to increase their possessions, want to know that their neighbours won't attack them in their sleep. Examples of this are shown in *A Wrinkle in Time, Little Women, Hansel and Gretel, Where the Red Fern Grows, Tom Sawyer, A Christmas Carol, Charlotte's Web* and *The Wizard of Oz*.

The next level in Maslow's hierarchy is the level of **love and belonging**. Stories that deal with the strongest desires at this level are often romances, but they could also be about a family that sticks together, about the team that works as a unit instead of independently, the lonely being drawn in. They can also be negative: the father abandons the impoverished family, the bride is jilted at the altar, or the black sheep leaves his family for greener pastures. Characters whose desires are in this level want to be loved. Examples include *Romeo and Juliet, King Lear, Pride and Prejudice, Twilight, Outlander, Jane Eyre, The Notebook, The Time Traveller's Wife, The Princess Bride, The Velveteen Rabbit* and *Winnie the Pooh*.

The next level is the level of **esteem**. Characters here are driven by what others think of them and what they think of themselves. They could also want fame or notoriety. Conversely, a character could have strong convictions that go against the crowd. Characters here stick up for their beliefs or cower behind others. Characters with desires at this level may want to become popular or famous. Other characters may also want to stand alone against the crowd and fight for their beliefs. Examples include *The Women, Are You There, God, It's Me, Margaret, Harriet the Spy, To Kill a Mockingbird, The Perks of Being a Wallflower, The Valley of the Dolls, The Help, My Antonia* and *The Divine Secrets of the Ya-Ya Sisterhood*.

**Self-actualization** is at the top of the hierarchy. At this last level, needs are the hardest to achieve. In some interpretations of Maslow's theory, this could include transcendent needs, when a character's biggest goal is to help others reach their potential. Characters here are often driven by their compassion, empathy and altruism. Additionally, at this level, characters could have a drive to fulfil cognitive curiosities, educate themselves and grow in understanding. Characters at this level could also be driven to be creative and artistic, creating beauty, symmetry or order. A person or a character whose needs are fulfilled at this level is said by Maslow to be 'self-actualized' (but a self-actualized character is a boring one). Examples include *Les Misérables, Silas Marner, Jonathan Livingston Seagull, The Hunchback of Notre Dame, The Picture of Dorian Gray, The Gift of the Magi, The Little Prince*.

# Needs, desire and conflict

Maslow's theory goes on to suggest that if our lower-level needs are not met, we will feel anxious and upset. Rightfully, these lower needs must be taken care of first before the others can be attended to. But it is possible, in the complex human brain, for us to pursue several motivations from different levels of the hierarchy at the same time.

This is what happens in *The Hunger Games*. From the beginning, readers are immediately drawn in to Katniss's opening struggle of caring for her family despite poverty and hunger. As the story progresses and Katniss displays more opportunities to fight, not only for survival but also to overcome the 'monsters' designing the games, her story becomes more compelling. Additionally, she has two love interests, Gale and Peeta, who help her in her fight for survival but divide her heart and loyalties. These divisions are often mutually exclusive. She has to keep her family safe, yet stand up against tyranny and risk her life. She wants to return to her life at Gale's side, but Peeta's devotion to her is disarming. She literally fights for her life in the Hunger Games arena and is required to kill people she cares for.

Yet in all of these conflicts, Katniss stays cool. She is brave, determined and admirable. Readers root for her because of her struggle and because of her inner virtues, and because she has to make some crazy, tough choices.

A character's needs should be *conflicting*. The main character should have to make a tough choice – to have security or to feed the starving around him? Does he win the race or follow his religious convictions? Does he remain a lonely, embittered miser or humble himself and celebrate Christmas? It is through these mutually exclusive needs that the conflicts become more real, the tension increases and your poor, tortured reader can't help but turn the page to find out what happens next.

Emma Woodhouse's needs are on the upper levels: she needs to solve the problems of others. She needs to be in charge of her little world. The climactic moment in her story is when she realizes that she has failed and she has to change the way she views herself and Mr Knightley. Frodo Baggins's biggest need is to destroy the ring (an issue of morality or of safety) and his needs conflict with his personal preference of staying at home. Romeo and Juliet's biggest need is satisfying their teenage lust, which conflicts with their families' need for them to uphold traditions. Each of these characters' conflicts come out of these contrasting needs and drive the story forward.

## Identifying need levels

Think of four main characters from your favourite films, novels and plays. Identify which level of need dictated their desires. Notice that characters in fairy tales often stick to the bottom two, while characters in some stories go up to the top of the triangle.

# Workshop

In reviewing all your notes, consider your story so far.

- List as many needs as your main character will have, on every level of Maslow's hierarchy. Be as thorough as possible. If you wish, you could research Maslow's hierarchy of needs further and apply what you discover to your character.
- From this list of needs, look at those that will cause a conflict for your main character. Then identify the two that are the most mutually exclusive. Which two seem to go against each other?
- Now list as many scenes as you can that would put your character in a position to choose one need over another. You are looking for conflict. The more conflict you have, the more interesting your story will be.
- Then choose which need will win. Your character will have to make a tough choice at some point in the story. You want their choice to be a costly one, the only one that will make the most sense, and if possible, a permanent one – one that allows for a change.
- Finally, work out how your story will end so that the conflicts are resolved in some way. You will probably want to rewrite it later.

## Where to next?

*Your protagonist needs supporting characters to help tell the story, and the next chapter will help you develop additional characters that are as real and vivid as the main character.*

# 9

## Additional characters

The main character in your story can't tell his story alone. His biggest goals need to be accomplished and he can't do it without companions, friends, counsellors, distractors, assistants and possibly a love interest. In your main character's quest, he will make mistakes, seek advice, get distracted, forget who he is, slip into the antagonist's hands, and ultimately make a difficult choice between two mutually exclusive needs. Everyone who has journeyed on this quest with him will have an opinion on this choice and will either help or hinder him as he succeeds or fails.

Because of this heavy responsibility, supporting characters need to be as thoroughly drawn as the main character. They need to be real. As with the main character, you can make them real by going through the four stages of character development: archetype, basic description, characterization and desires.

Gustave Flaubert

*'You forget everything. The hours slip by. You travel in your chair through centuries you seem to see before you, your thoughts are caught up in the story, dallying with the details or following the course of the plot, you enter into characters, so that it seems as if it were your own heart beating beneath their costumes.'*

The supporting characters are the harmonizing voices in the song sung by your main character. Yes, the story is about *him*, the protagonist. But there is rarely the story that can be told well without the supporting cast. With the support cast at his side, the main character can explain his quest, sound off, gain protection, garner wisdom and get distracted. The readers need the cast, too. They need to see your main character from all sides – sides that his sister, his mother, his girlfriend, his employer, his father, his best friend and his dog can only see from their point of view. Unlike the main character, readers are not obliged to love the supporting characters. You are free to make them obnoxious, hilarious, angry, adorable or pitiful. They can exaggerate the best and the worst of your main character, they can reflect the themes you want to convey, they can distort the values of the main character and reveal more discoveries about the story.

# Supporting-character archetypes

As we have seen in the previous chapter, archetypes originated in the ancient Greek theatre, when characters were not drawn nearly as deeply as they are today and often it was only an archetype that told the audience what to expect. In these early plays there would be a fool, for instance, or a sage or a love interest. If you haven't thought about your supporting cast yet, you can use the following list of supporting character archetypes to ignite your imagination as to which ones you need to tell your story. If you already have an idea of who else is helping your main character, the archetypes may help you see their roles with fresh insight. Regardless, your story will need at least three supporting characters.

This list of supporting-character archetypes differs from the list given for the protagonist simply because, generally speaking, the supporting characters react to the protagonist. The supporting character's job is to help or hinder the accomplishment of the protagonist's goal and take a side in the choice of the two mutually exclusive needs. The archetypes include the conscience, the tempter, the buddy, the sceptic, the emotionalist and the rationalist.

## THE CONSCIENCE

The conscience is the person in the story who will speak wisdom to the main character, whether they listen to it or not. Sometimes this character is an authority figure, like a teacher or a coach, a sage or a Jedi Master. Sometimes it's an inferior, like a younger sibling, a cricket or an angel resting on a shoulder. Often in stories, the conscience's wisdom is ignored and the relationship is strained until the main character gets an epiphany and realizes that the conscience was right all along. Examples of conscience characters include Jiminy Cricket, Wendy Darling, Linus van Pelt, Gandalf, the Ghosts of Christmases Past, Present and Future, Jane Bennet, Glinda the Good Witch, Mrs Weston, Obi-Wan Kenobi and Aslan.

## THE TEMPTER

The tempter tries to convince the main character *not* to pursue his goals. The tempter's arguments may be valid and altruistic but they can also be deceptive and selfish, possibly taking advantage of our hero. The tempter can betray the protagonist and really be an antagonist, or the tempter can just be a distraction. Examples of the tempter include Gollum, Edmund Pevensie, Dill Harris, Mr Wickham, Mr Willoughby and Frank Churchill.

## THE BUDDY

The buddy is the sidekick or the best friend who is with the main character through thick and thin. Buddies are often the most loved characters in a story because of their devotion to the main character. A buddy is the one who offers encouragement, who carries the protagonist's stuff, the wingman and the designated driver. At some point there's usually a rift between the main character and the buddy and then the main character realizes he can't accomplish his goals alone. If there's going to be hugging in your story, it's with the buddy. Examples of the buddy include Samwise Gamgee, Gale, Harriet Smith, Dr Watson, Snoopy, Huckleberry Finn, Fozzie Bear, Roger Sterling and Chewbacca.

## THE SCEPTIC

The sceptic is the character who doesn't believe in the main character's quest. For whatever reason, the sceptic will discourage the main character from even starting. Sometimes this is a parent not believing in the teen with the big ideas. Sometimes it's the kids at school. Regardless, the sceptic plays an important role. By confronting the sceptic, the main character often grows more determined. If the relationship between the main character and the sceptic is a tight one, then the actions of the protagonist could be costly to the sceptic. Examples of the sceptic character are Mr Woodhouse, Lucy van Pelt, Ron Weasley, 'Bones' McCoy, George Costanza and Han Solo.

## THE EMOTIONALIST

The emotionalist is the character who adds to the story through their extreme emotional involvement with the main character. They may be the crazy ex-girlfriend who shows up at the wrong time wanting to 'talk'. They may be a joker or a prankster, playing the classic comic relief. Their emotions may go the other way, too: for example, overreacting to failure, freezing in fear during an attack or saying the wrong thing at the wrong time out of nerves. The emotionalist can be fun to read about but may also come across as annoying. Examples include Mrs Bennet, Lydia Bennet, Jay Gatsby, Donald Duck, Phoebe from *Friends* and the Cowardly Lion.

## THE RATIONALIST

The rationalist is the 'brains of the operation'. This character has a lot to say about the quest of the main character and uses logic and reason to either help or hinder him in pursuit of his goals. The rationalist is a good character to bounce ideas off and can be a natural place from which the facts of the story can surface. The main character could depend on the rationalist for practical help or wisdom. Unlike the conscience, the rationalist gives practical rather than moral or ethical advice. Examples of rationalists include Fitzwilliam Darcy, George Knightley, Jem Finch, Aragorn and Mr Spock.

# Supporting characters in action

As you study supporting characters in various stories, you will see that each of them reacts and responds to the needs and desires of the main character in different ways. If they disagree with or discourage the protagonist, there is opportunity for conflict, which drives the story. If they agree with and encourage the protagonist, there is a united sense of purpose and a willingness to overcome obstacles, which also drives the story.

To examine the archetypes more closely, let's look at who surrounded the decisions, directives and dalliances of Mrs Katie Scarlett O'Hara Hamilton Kennedy Butler – the ruthless, driven survivor of Margaret Mitchell's sweeping saga *Gone with the Wind* (1936).

## THE CONSCIENCE

The first important supporting character we meet in *Gone with the Wind* is Mammy. Mammy is Scarlett's house slave who raised her. From the first scene, when Scarlett is preparing for the picnic at Twelve Oaks, we see Mammy adjusting Scarlett's corset, covering her bare shoulders and instructing her not to be too gluttonous. According to Mammy, a girl with a big appetite isn't likely to get a husband:

> '*I is told ya and told ya that you can always tell a lady by the way she eat in front of folks like a bird. And I ain't aimin' for you to go to Mr John Wilkenson's and eat like a field hand and gobble like a hog!*'

For a slave, Mammy is bold with Scarlett. She immediately takes the role of Scarlett's conscience and continues to play this role throughout the book. If only Scarlett would listen to her.

## THE BUDDY

Later, at the party, the readers (or viewers) meet Melanie Wilkes. Melanie is the exact opposite of Scarlett. Where Scarlett is flirtatious, Melanie is modest. Where Scarlett is determined to have what she wants, Melanie is content. Scarlett is conniving, even to the point of marrying Charles Hamilton, Melanie's brother, out of spite. Melanie is devoted to her husband, Ashley. And Scarlett is duplicitous; she has no trouble sidling up to Melanie just so that she can get her claws into this same man. Melanie can't imagine any of Scarlett's actions being selfish. Melanie is a buddy for Scarlett as they move to Atlanta, mourn the death of Charles and try to survive the Yankee invasion, but Melanie is, unbeknown to her, a rival. Scarlett's obsession is Ashley Wilkes. She will do *anything* for the love of Ashley.

## THE SCEPTIC

We can't forget Rhett Butler, who is more like Scarlett O'Hara than any other character. He discovers Scarlett's ultimate desire early in the story and it is from this knowledge that he exploits his relationship with Scarlett and Melanie. Perhaps the reason Scarlett is repulsed by him is that he is so much like her. He questions Scarlett's every decision. He rescues her repeatedly, but he always reminds her that he's doing it because it's the right thing to do, not because she deserves it. Rhett is a sceptic *and* a rationalist and he goes back and forth between helping Scarlett and hindering her in her quest for survival and her quest for Ashley's love.

## THE TEMPTER

Ashley Wilkes could be Scarlett's tempter, whether he admits it or not. His actions have put it in her head that he loves her and it's this hope of a happy union that drives her throughout the long book. His obligations are to the Confederates, to Melanie and to whatever honour he can piece together through the rubble of post-Civil War Georgia. His relationship to Scarlett is always tied to Melanie and it's a complicated one.

## THE EMOTIONALIST

Gerald O'Hara, Scarlett's sisters, Prissy and Aunt Pittypat are Scarlett's emotionalists. Their flightiness and incompetence drive Scarlett to assume leadership of the family. When she does, they see Scarlett as insensitive and brutal. They play an important role in the story because they highlight Scarlett's drive and raise the stakes: Scarlett has somehow to feed and clothe all of them after their fortunes are destroyed.

## Using the archetypes

From the list of supporting character archetypes, think how your own additional characters could fit those roles. If you need to combine a role, as for example, with Rhett Butler who is Scarlett's sceptic *and* rationalist, you can. Write down any insights you may have on this character development.

## Write about your supporting characters

Return to your notes from the last chapter about the desires of your protagonist, then free write how each of your supporting characters a) disagrees with or opposes your main character and b) how each of your supporting characters agrees with or supports your main character.

# Basic description

Your supporting cast must be as real as your main character. Every detail you can include will be helpful. These characters didn't spring out of nowhere. They have pasts, they have a history with the main character and they have their own identities. The difference is that the supporting characters are not the star. Instead, they revolve around the centre of this story's universe – your protagonist.

In this section, ask the same questions of basic description for the supporting cast as you did for your protagonist. Remember that every supporting character has to be deeply involved in the progression of the story (there was no need, for example, to give significant detail to the red-headed twins who go with Scarlett to the picnic, especially when we find out later that they died at Gettysburg. Sorry, Tarletons!)

Key idea

To keep your characters organized, consider using a spreadsheet with all their important information on it, so that you can refer to it often.

## Workshop

Answer the following questions for each supporting character. As you make your choices, lean towards the opposite of the choices you made for your main character, if you can, for the sake of potential conflicts. (Conflicts are good, and you want as much opportunity for them as you can get.)

1 What are their names? Choose their names in relation to the main characters. You want to avoid repetitive sounds or the same numbers of syllables. The more varied you make the names (within reason – you want them to fit the setting well), the easier it will be on the reader. (How many readers of *The Lord of the Rings* have got Sauron and Saruman confused?)

2 How old are they? What is their birth order?

3 What is their economic station?

4 What does each of them look like? Distinguishing characteristics?

5 How do these characters compare to your main character in intelligence? Are they academically smart? Street smart? Imaginative? Socially savvy?

6 What is the education level of each of your characters? What are their talents and hobbies? Are they healthy? Do they have any bad habits?

7 In your previous notes, have you observed something in someone else that you could use for any of these characters? It might be the way they walked, a specific outfit or a catchphrase.

8 How are they connected to the main character?

# Characterization

The principle described by Robert McKee above means that the characterization of your supporting characters must be fully fleshed out. We do this in much the same way that we have sculpted our main character. Tools like the Meyers–Briggs Type Indicator or Temperament Theory are a good start. Also, by comparing and contrasting the inner personalities of our supporting cast with our main character, we can see more of who they are. They must have preferences and personalities, desires and motivations, possibly even be worthy of a story set around them too.

## Focus point

You may find the exercises in this section to be redundant. If so, don't do them. The point is to sculpt each character from all sides. When you think you have thoroughly created them, move on.

## Write as a supporting character

Do a free write, in the voice of a supporting character, that describes the main character. Explain what irritates and vexes the supporting character about this relationship.

# The four cornerstones

Review your notes on the four cornerstones of character from Chapter 8: the Secret, the Flaw, the Fear and the Quirk. How do your supporting characters display these? How do they compare and contrast with your main character?

# Your characters in action

Imagine all your supporting cast at a casual dinner party at a local restaurant. The waiter makes a huge gaffe – spilling food or overcharging everyone or bringing the meal late and cold. Write for ten minutes on how each of your characters would handle that situation. What would they say to the others? How would they treat the waiter? What do they do when the manager's response is unsatisfactory?

# Workshop

If you need to, review the 20 personality questions repeated from the first workshop in Chapter 8 for the protagonist. See whether, by answering these questions, your supporting cast is in contrast with the personality of the main character.

1  Is your character flighty or dependable?
2  Is your character warm and open or cold and hard to know?
3  Does your character exhibit fairness or does he cheat?
4  Is he smart or below average intellectually?
5  Is he culturally aware or ignorant of the world around him?
6  Is he conscious of others or oblivious to others?
7  Does he trust his friends and family or does he suspect they will hurt him?
8  Does he work hard at all he does or is he lazy and does he cut corners?

9 Is he secure in who he is or self-conscious?

10 Does he relax easily or is he uptight?

11 Are his emotions on an even keel or does he fly off the handle?

12 Does he have a lot of energy for physical and emotional challenges or does he weaken easily?

13 Does he pick up non-verbal cues well or is his only perception what people say?

14 Does he anger easily? If so, about what? Or is he patient and kind with others?

15 Is he a problem solver and practical or does he value more impractical things?

16 Does he want to learn more about life or is he not particularly curious?

17 Is he sociable and wiling to talk to and meet others or does he prefer solitude?

18 Is he creative? Does he see things others don't? Or is he confined to his own traditions and rules?

19 Is he well organized and orderly in his surroundings or thoughtless and cluttered?

20 Does he find people energizing or does he find time alone more energizing?

 ## Your characters' needs

Review the notes you made in Chapter 8 on Maslow's hierarchy of needs. For each of your supporting cast, determine what their biggest needs are. Free write on this and notice how these needs may oppose the needs of the main character. Note any conflict you see – this will make your story better.

## Where to next?

*The antagonist – the opposing force – in your novel is just as important as your protagonist, and the next chapter explores how to develop this character as fully as possible to make your story more powerful.*

# 10

## The antagonist

Who is the hero of your story? Could the answer depend on who you ask?

Your story in this note-taking phase is probably focused on just one main character – their trials, their objectives and their happy ending. But there is another character, another force, another story within this story. Your story is also about how your antagonist – with their own objectives and backstory – actively prevents your main character from fulfilling his quest.

Your antagonist has just as significant a purpose in the story as your protagonist. This purpose is to deceive, misguide, manipulate, discourage and stop the protagonist from achieving his goal. This antagonist can be as simple as a meddling mother-in-law, as complex as the Evil Empire or as iconic as Dracula, but it is the opposing force that must be in your story. The more fully developed it is, the more interesting your story becomes.

Bram Stoker, *Dracula*

> '*The last I saw of Count Dracula was his kissing his hand to me, with a red light of triumph in his eyes, and with a smile that Judas in hell might be proud of.*'

Along with providing an opposing force, the antagonist also helps the story along in several other ways. His opposition clarifies the mission of the protagonist, reveals the character of the protagonist during setbacks, determines the mutually exclusive desires of the protagonist, and unifies the protagonist with the other characters on the mission. A fully formed, living, breathing antagonist will generate sympathy from the reader for the main character and will, in a sense, invite the reader to come along with the hero, saying, 'Let's get this guy together!'

Antagonists though, can be a varied bunch. Each type of antagonist reacts to the protagonist differently.

# The equal or benign antagonist

Your antagonist could be a classmate or a teammate – say a Josie Pye or a Gilbert Blythe to your Anne Shirley – someone close to your protagonist but who can't handle the competition, believes he deserves more or wants the girl. If that's the case, evaluate the lives of the two opposing characters. Make sure that the antagonist is formidable enough to keep the struggle going. The story shouldn't come easily to either of them. What do they need to have in common? What is it in their lives that contrasts? How can you make their competition unique?

Your antagonist could also be a benign force such as a nameless institution. Say your main character wants to get into Oxford or play for the New England Patriots. If that's the case, the rules and restrictions set up by these institutions are impersonal hurdles. And the more hurdles your character faces, the better. If this is the case, make sure that the obstacles you create are alive, not sterile. That mean and unfeeling college recruiter must be a fully formed character, too.

# The evil antagonist

What do Dracula, Moriarty, Sauron and the White Witch have in common? They are all evil in the same way. They are narcissistic, sociopathic, mentally ill or megalomaniac. They could also be chemically imbalanced, traumatized, abused, abandoned, neglected, deprived, frustrated or angry. They could also be under a spell, cursed, undead or out to seek their revenge. Because of their past, perhaps, they lack the ability to think rationally. And they believe that they are entitled to have victory. They are also often delusional and immoral and may not follow the rules, play fairly or be completely honest in their dealings with the protagonist. Because they are so very *bad,* they get to cheat, lie, steal, kidnap and use magical Turkish Delight to get whatever they want. They're also *great fun to write.*

Most importantly, they also have this in common: they don't see themselves as a villain. As you develop the antagonist, you will need to understand why the villain believes what he's doing is right and good. You will need to work through why he believes that opposing the protagonist is a good thing and brings life. If this were *his* story, what assumptions would he have, what lies would he believe and what actions would he take to meet *his* goals? What justifications does the villain have for the actions that he takes against the protagonist? He must *almost* succeed. What does that look like?

Yet, even the worst people have private lives. They care about something. What is it that your antagonist really cares about? Even if the entire backstory is never mentioned in the story, as the author you need to know this. The more you know and understand about your antagonist, the more fully you can create him to be hated.

# The non-human antagonist

Sometimes the forces of antagonism are not embodied by just a bad guy in a black hat, a vampire or a green-skinned woman with a penchant for spells. Sometimes the opposing force in your story is abstract, unpredictable or unrecognizable. Sometimes it's something inside the hero, or the expectations of others. Your antagonist could be that football team from the other side of town, a wild animal or a deadly disease, but regardless of *what* it is, your reader needs to have a clear picture of just how fully it opposes your hero. Non-human villains may be much harder to write but a skilled writer can pull it off with vivid description and detail.

Antagonists like this are complicated. If your antagonist is not human, take extra care to understand it inside and out. Plan for scenes when this opposing force shows its strength and terrifies the protagonist. Clarify the consequences to everyone in the story if the antagonist were to win. The non-human antagonists can often propel a suspenseful, thrilling story and if written well, this can scare or intrigue the reader.

 Key idea

Whatever type of antagonist you choose for your story – equal, benign, evil or non-human – make it as multidimensional and powerful as possible, so that your readers will hate it all the more. This is a guaranteed way to keep them reading long after they should have turned out the lights and gone to bed.

Like the protagonist, an antagonist must be fully drawn – as the author you must know what motivates your villain to make the choices he makes. Use the previous exercises in Chapters 8 and 9, such as the four cornerstones or Maslow's hierarchy of needs, to determine what this is. Unlike the protagonist, the antagonist will not have two opposing desires. He has only one – to defeat the hero so that he can have his way, whatever that way is.

In the creation of the antagonist, the four cornerstones are far more important than to the protagonist. We want the reader to see hints of these, even if the protagonist is not aware of them. These four cornerstones can be worked to maximize conflict and tension. The more secrets that the antagonist keeps from the protagonist and uses them as an 'ace up the sleeve', the more sympathy will be generated for the protagonist.

Consider carefully what is going on behind the scenes. Why does the antagonist behave in the way they do, why do they make the choices they make? Is this a game and is each move a strategic one? Why?

# Developing your antagonist

Return to the exercises on the protagonist in Chapter 8 and apply them to the development of your antagonist. Once you know the type of character you have in mind – the archetype – write out the basic description, then character and finally desires. Look specifically for ways in which this character development opposes the actions and beliefs of the protagonist.

## Workshop

In as many ten-minute increments as you need, answer the following questions about your antagonist.

- What does your antagonist not see about himself that the protagonist does?
- How can the protagonist use this to his advantage?
- Now reverse the question: what flaw does the protagonist have that the antagonist notices and can use to defeat him?
- What perceptions does the antagonist have of the protagonist? Is the protagonist a true threat? How is this demonstrated in the story?
- What habit or lie does the antagonist use to prevent others from achieving their goals? How does he do this?
- How does your antagonist react when his flaws are revealed? What other reactions does the antagonist have towards the protagonist, especially when he makes gains in his quest?
- Is there an inconsistency between the true identity of your antagonist and the image he is portraying?
- How longstanding is the relationship between the protagonist and the antagonist? Are there grudges here? Bitterness? Anger? Revenge? Injustice?
- What permanent result will occur if the antagonist fails in his attempt to hinder the protagonist in his goals? What will it cost the antagonist if the protagonist succeeds?

*Now that you have a clear idea of your cast of characters, the next chapter explores how to decide on your narrator and point of view – in other words, who will tell your story.*

# 11

## Narrative voice and point of view

The narrative voice is the connecting glue between reader, writer and story. The story's biggest character *can* be the narrator or the point-of-view (POV) character, but it doesn't have to be. Sometimes another character's point of view is the most interesting. You've created your cast of characters and you may have an inkling of what exactly happens in your story. The question only you can answer is: *who can tell it best?*

The choice of the perfect narrator can add richness to the story you are telling, and it may not be the protagonist. Whoever it is, the narrative voice is the first voice the reader encounters and it must be interesting, unique and have insight into the story that no other character would have. As the first act progresses, the reader will trust the narrator for the rest of the 'ride'.

Harper Lee, *To Kill a Mockingbird*

'*When he was nearly thirteen, my brother Jem got his arm badly broken at the elbow. When it healed, and Jem's fears of never being able to play football were assuaged, he was seldom self-conscious about his injury.*'

 F. Scott Fitzgerald, *The Great Gatsby*

'*In my younger and more formidable years my father gave me some advice that I've been turning over in my mind ever since. "Whenever you feel like criticizing anyone," he told me, "just remember that all the people in this world haven't had the advantages that you've had."*'

The first voice in the story is the one that the reader often develops the strongest attachment to, whether are not they are the main character. Scout Finch and Nick Carraway became two of the most intriguing narrators in American literature because they got to tell their sides of their own stories as well as the ostensible main story.

Scout suggested that the story was about her brother Jem's broken arm. From the opening lines, this story sounds like a simple one, a child's tale. But *To Kill a Mockingbird* is about far more than just what it was that happened on a dark sidewalk that left a boy unconscious and helpless.

Similarly, *The Great Gatsby* is far more than a tale of one summer in the 1920s on Long Island. Through the story, Nick Carraway observed the behaviour of Jay Gatsby and Daisy and judged, rightly or wrongly, the consequences of their actions.

The narrative voices in both of these books, Nick's and Scout's, were chosen, arguably, for their specific relationship to the main character and their unique perspective on the plot. In *To Kill a Mockingbird* and *The Great Gatsby,* neither narrative character was the most important person in the story, but these particular points of view gave value and beauty to the story itself. Scout and Nick, as characters, were elemental to the themes of the book. Any other narrator would have weakened other aspects of the story.

# The function of narrative voice

When you are deciding on your narrative voice or point of view, you need to decide what you want it to do. Do you want it to fit the genre or enhance the plot or setting? Do you want it to show the relationships with other characters or emphasize the narrator's own character? You may want to choose your narrative voice to fit the level of intimacy you want to give the reader.

## FITTING THE GENRE

How does genre play in narrative voice? Happier endings need happier voices. The voice should be consistent with what the reader should expect in the story. Both *To Kill a Mockingbird* and *The Great Gatsby* are hardly happy stories and their narrators know this.

## ENHANCING THE PLOT

Could you imagine *Gone with the Wind* from Melanie's point of view or *Winnie the Pooh* from Eyeore's? Could *The Hunger Games* be told from Gale's point of view or *Emma* from Mr Elton's? Choose your narrator because he has a fresh take on the story or because he has the most to lose. Or maybe he's innocent and becomes enlightened, as Scout did. Or maybe he's judgemental and points out folly to the readers, like Nick.

## ENHANCING THE SETTING

In *To Kill a Mockingbird*, Scout thinks she knows her world – the neighbourhood, her home, her brother and her father. She has an innocent sheen about her even though she lives in a world full of injustice. The Alabama of the 1930s was unkind to many. Scout's eyes slowly open to the ugliness around her and she depends on her father to explain it to her.

Nick, also, is a creature of his setting. He has expectations of what 1920s Long Island should be. He is conflicted when comparing his own life of comparative ease and luxury with Gatsby's excesses. His voice explains his conflict to the reader. His social circles were not as gilded as they seemed. Other narrators, even other characters in the story, may not have been as affected by their setting as Nick and Scout are. Would a story told from Atticus's point of view capture the simplicity of the setting that Scout's did? Would Jay's account of his adventures even be interesting?

## SHOWING RELATIONSHIPS WITH OTHER CHARACTERS

Nick and Scout make great narrators, not because the story is about them but because they are close to the main character and they reflect his importance. Through their experiences, they make the greatness of the biggest character more human. They translate the biggest character's actions and speech to the reader. In their dealings with the other characters, our narrator goes back and forth between sympathy and frustration as the story progresses. Scout's response to Atticus and Nick's to Gatsby are what make the story.

## SHOWING THE NARRATOR'S CHARACTER

The narrator is able to express his values and perspective to the reader in ways that the other characters can't. The narrator's emotions, prejudices, passions and opinions – innocence in the case of Scout and cynicism in the case of Nick – enrich their account. The narrator may have secrets that the main character doesn't know, flaws that torment both of them or desires counter to the hero's. The characterization of the narrator (from the exercise on character traits – the Fear, the Secret, the Flaw and the Quirk – in Chapter 8) should be considered when choosing and developing the narrative voice.

## EXPRESSING THE LEVEL OF INTIMACY

Novels are most frequently written from one of four points of view: first person, third person, multiple and omniscient. Each perspective has advantages and disadvantages for the reader and for the writer. These points of view start with the most intimate – first person – and decrease in intimacy as more and more characters' thoughts are added to the story. Both Scout and Nick are first-person stories and, as a result, the reader *becomes* them for the duration of the story. Some stories are enhanced by this; others are not. But each point of view is worth understanding. Point of view *must* remain consistent throughout the book. It's isn't fair to the reader, or the characters, to start with Scout's story and end up with Miz Stephanie Crawford's.

# First-person narration

## William Zinsser

*'I almost always urge people to write in the first person ... writing is an act of ego and you might as well admit it.'*

Writers may naturally gravitate toward a first-person point of view in their stories, not for literary merit and storytelling value but for the sake of being the hero themselves. It's no wonder that first-person stories are so common in literature. But these first-person narratives vary; some are in the main character's voice, as in *The Fault in Our Stars* and *The Adventures of Huckleberry Finn,* while others are the voice of a spectator or witness to the events in the story, like *Moby Dick*.

The first-person narrative has to start out strongly. Here are some famous first lines that demonstrate the first-person point of view.

- *Moby Dick:* 'Call me Ishmael.'
- *The Fault in Our Stars:* 'Late in the winter of my seventeenth year, my mother decided I was depressed, presumably because I rarely left the house, spent quite a lot of time in my bed, read the same book over and over, ate infrequently, and devoted quite a bit of my abundant free time to thinking about death.'
- *The Adventures of Huckleberry Finn:* 'You don't know about me, without you have read a book by the name of The Adventures of Tom Sawyer, but that ain't no matter.'
- *The Hunger Games:* 'When I wake up, the other side of the bed is cold.'
- *The Catcher in the Rye:* 'If you really want to hear about it, the first thing you'll probably want to know is where I was born, and what my lousy childhood was like, and how my parents were occupied and all before they had me, and all that David Copperfield kind of crap, but I don't feel like going into it, if you want to know the truth.'

The first advantage of using first person is that the story is not from the voice of the author but from the voice of a character. A strong first-person narrator automatically places the reader deep into the story. First person more easily allows for the suspension of disbelief: it gives credibility to the account of the story. The first-person narrator is now a new friend, a new confidant, or someone who has seen and done intriguing things. With first person, the reader is often engaged from the beginning with an intimate, believable immediacy.

A first-person narrator may act as a spoiler because the reader concludes early on that he or she survived the story (a comforting thought in *The Hunger Games*). However, other first-person stories have been written from a dead character's point of view or by the spirit of a deceased person. Skilful writers can pull this off with the element of surprise.

The disadvantages of first-person narration include the limited perspective. The reader has access to only the narrator's actions, emotions, conclusions, suppositions and knowledge. If something significant happens in the story, the narrator has to witness it or be told about it in a convincing and thoughtful way.

In a first-person narrative, the appearance of the narrator is tricky to describe. Many authors have had their narrators look in mirrors or glass windows to see their reflection. If that device isn't used, then other characters' dialogue must reveal this information. Skilled writers can pull this off without making it seem contrived.

## Third-person narration

 Victoria Mixon, *The Art and Craft of Fiction*

'... first person got kind of beaten to death over the millennia, so these days we use third person for everything but the most specific of situations.'

The third-person narrative removes the author's ego from the storytelling, pulls back on the intimacy between reader and main character, and can still show the viewpoint of either the strongest character in the story or someone close to him.

Here are some examples of first lines that start the story in the third person:

- *Go Tell It on the Mountain:* 'Everyone had always said that John would be a preacher when he grew up, just like his father.'
- *The Member of the Wedding:* 'It happened that green and crazy summer when Frankie was twelve years old.'
- *The Giver:* 'It was almost December, and Jonas was beginning to be frightened.'
- *The Voyage of the* Dawn Treader: 'There was a boy called Eustace Clarence Scrubb, and he almost deserved it.'
- *The Old Man and the Sea*: 'He was an old man who fished alone in a skiff in the Gulf Stream and he had gone eighty-four days now without taking a fish.'
- *Middlemarch:* 'Miss Brooke had that kind of beauty which seems to be thrown into relief by poor dress.'

Third person is the most common point of view in fiction. Third person allows the reader to feel as if they are in on the intimate life of the main character, but in an over-the-shoulder kind of way. While this still allows for a deep attachment to the main character, there's still a bit of distance between the reader and protagonist. Third person works well with stories that are not so inwardly focused or contemplative. Third person is the most conventional narrative voice and should be a default setting for beginning writers.

In a third-person narrative, anything can happen to anyone. Had *The Hunger Games* been written in the third person, Katniss's success wouldn't have been as obvious and the immediacy of her peril would have been lost. The open-endedness of a third-person narrative raises the stakes for the main characters and allows the author more freedom.

Third person also allows for a separation between the story and the reader. This is helpful if the story sculptor wants the reader to be aware of other characters, specific actions and exposition that may occur in settings from which the main character is absent. This also creates freedom for the storyteller.

In third-person narrative, the reader passes judgement, for better or worse, on the main characters more easily. Sometimes an author *doesn't* want to generate sympathy and the distance between the reader and the main characters can encourage this emotional distance. Appearances are also easier to describe in the third person. An author can express his image of all the characters more precisely, without resorting to looking in mirrors or other tricks. Third person narrative also sets a tone that is distinct from the voice of the other characters. This is helpful in writing humorous stories in which the main characters' antics are fodder for mockery.

 Focus point

Second-person narrative is rarely used in fiction because of the difficulty in telling a story from the reader's point of view. Second-person point of view uses the pronoun 'you': 'You went to the shop and bought grapes and cheese. The old man saw you and asked you if you knew the time. You said you didn't.' There are successful novels that have succeeded with second person, but authors usually avoid it; *Choose Your Own Adventure* books for middle-grade boys can successfully pull it off.

# The omniscient narrator

 Victoria Mixon, *The Art and Craft of Fiction*

*'But omniscient narrator is so much more specialized than even the other specialized techniques, and yet so commonly misunderstood and missed and (dare I be so dark?) abused that there's no point in attempting it if we're not going to do it right.'*

Omniscient point of view means getting into the heads of all the characters to tell one story. It's no wonder that the most successful omniscient narrative voices come from sagas that are complicated, long and breathtaking in scope. The first lines of these books can't give an indication of the vast narrative that is in store for the reader.

Here are some examples of first lines from books that use the omniscient point of view. Of course, this isn't revealed in the lines themselves. But the books are all long, epic sagas. Omniscient point of view needs the space to tell the story from everyone's mind.

- *Jonathan Strange and Mr Norrell:* 'Some years ago, in the city of York, there was a society of magicians.'
- *The Fellowship of the Ring:* 'When Mr Bilbo Baggins of Bag End announced that he would shortly be celebrating his eleventy-first birthday with a party of special magnificence, there was much talk and excitement in Hobbiton.'
- *Game of Thrones:* '"We should start back," Gared urged as the woods began to grow dark around them.'
- *Discworld:* 'In a distant and second-hand set of dimensions, in an astral plane that was never meant to fly, the curling star mists waver and part ...'
- *Watership Down:* 'The primroses were over.'
- *Les Misérables:* 'An hour before sunset, on the evening of a day in the beginning of October, 1815, a man travelling afoot entered the little town of D____.'

Omniscient point of view, which can also be called cinematic for its tendency to move around from head to head, allows the reader to know the thoughts and motivations of every significant character for the story. The omniscient third-person point of view gives a wide range of perspectives. The difficulty in omniscient point of view is keeping the reader from getting confused. The change from one point of view to another must be done skilfully and precisely, or the reader is distracted and confused. Poorly written *head-hopping* can muddy the intention of the story, confuse the reader and put in too much information. This technique is not therefore recommended for beginning writers.

# Victoria Mixon, *The Art and Craft of Fiction*

*'Devote yourself to a minimum of one year of conscientiously researching (finding, reading and analysing) only the most accomplished novels written in third-person omniscient, dissecting them POV switch by POV switch, looking for patterns, looking for relationship illuminations, looking for the ways in which the authors use the transition from one POV to another as a technique in-&-of itself to show the reader something they couldn't possibly have shown any other way.'*

Writing in omniscient point of view allows for the reader to have insight that the characters do not, but gives little attention to the inner drives of any one character. The reader, then, may not know who to root for or may not attach themselves to one character.

## Multiple points of view

A book with multiple points of view often has the best of all worlds. Potentially, it can have both the intimacy of first person and the flexibility of third person. The hopping from character to character is often done from chapter to chapter. If a writer considers each chapter as a brand new sub-novel within the novel, this could make the chapter more manageable and coherent. This method is less intimidating than the omniscient point of view but harder and more complicated than the other two. Writers who attempt to write in multiple points of view will have extra work to do: they will need to carefully sculpt the story in such a way that the reader is fully engaged with each point-of-view character.

The advantage of multiple points of view is that the story is seen through several characters, whose different insights, different interpretations, and different voices make the story richer. The reader has to choose whose voice seems the most credible and possibly most interesting. Unfortunately, the author has to work hard to make each separate narrative voice as distinct as possible. The reader should be able to ease into the point of view and not waste time figuring out who is in charge. Within a multiple point-of-view story, third person is far easier to follow than first person, although some writers have used tricks like fonts or styles to mark the change.

 ## A note on tense

Classical story structure requires that stories take place in the past tense. Narrative voices most often tell the story of what happened in the past, like explaining why Jem's arm is broken. Past tense is the easiest and most common tense to write in. However, present-tense stories telling us what is happening now create a sense of motion and urgency. This tense is difficult to pull off and, like omniscient point of view, should be wielded by writers who have mastered the simpler forms first.

# Choosing your narrative voice

Choosing the right tense, voice and point of view for your novel is important because it can enhance the story for your reader. However, you can always change your mind about the choice you initially made as you sculpt the novel. You may have new insights about the plot or characters that mean you need the narrative voice to have a different sound. That's what rewriting is for.

All the following exercises aim to encourage you to think about your narrative choice. If you have no idea who your narrator will be, then do them all. If you already know, then do only the ones that will help illuminate that character and his voice for you.

# Who should narrate?

Does one of your characters have the most to say about the others? Which one is the most observant, or the most secretive, perhaps? Which person's perspective will be the most interesting? What if you had all your characters in a room and they were all telling you what happened in this story? Whose take would be the most reliable? Who would be the most entertaining or the most animated? Write for ten minutes about this.

## Workshop

Are there any characters that may be a better beacon of illumination of your theme than the protagonist and that would make an interesting narrative voice? In this workshop you will look at all your characters in turn and write in the voice of each one before deciding which one should take the role of narrator.

The voice of the speaking character should fit their personality. Are they meticulous about detail? Easily offended? Romantic? Do you see any themes emerging?

- Review all your characters and do a ten-minute free write in each of their voices. Which one did you enjoy writing the most?
- Free write for ten minutes telling the story through that character's voice and note any insight you may have in this exercise.
- Return to the four cornerstones for each character (see Chapter 8). Of these four, which could be hidden from the reader? How would this shape the person you've chosen to be the narrator? Free write in that character's voice for ten minutes, playing around with the four cornerstones. You could start the story with, 'I am afraid of …' and begin telling the story. Do this for the other three cornerstones. Note any insight. Is there a tone that speaks out to you?

*In the next chapter we will be discussing how to build your story round the classic three-act structure, so that it has a clear beginning, middle and end.*

# 12

## The three-act structure

Storytellers who are not familiar with the concepts of three-act structure often create meandering, boring stories. By knowing the ins and outs of three-act structure and applying them to the story forming in your mind, your story will have an adequate pace and rise in tension and it will draw the reader towards the final conclusion. This basic story structure, in a nutshell, comprises three acts full of sequences and scenes that are all a series of causes and effects that make up the beginning, the middle and the end.

The exercises in this chapter will help you organize your ideas for your story into this three-act structure. Take all the time you need to create a beginning, a middle and an end. Keep these notes handy. You will be using them again in the next few chapters, which explain in more detail what requirements are needed for each act.

## Lemony Snicket

*'In this book, not only is there no happy ending, there is no happy beginning and very few happy things in the middle.'*

To continue the sculpture metaphor from earlier in this book, if you were really sculpting, say, Michaelangelo's *David*, then you would need to stay true to the form of the human body as you progressed. Your objective would be to create an accurate, recognizable and proportional body. In the art of classical sculpture, artists must stay true to the physio-biological laws of structure and form.

It is the same way with structure of a story. The 'rules' of a classic three-act story are the skeleton. The sequences are the specific sections, such as legs, arms and torso. The scenes are the specific parts of those parts – the ankle, the shin, the calf. The beats, or pulses of a scene, are the bones and muscles. All work together, for individual specific purposes for the sake of the whole to create a recognizable, predictable work of art.

## Robert McKee, *Story: Substance, Structure, Style, and the Principles of Screenwriting*

*'Classical design means a story built around an active protagonist who struggles against primarily external forces of antagonism to pursue his or her desire through continuous time, within a consistent and causally connected fictional reality, to a closed ending of absolute, irreversible change.'*

In McKee's definition, quoted above, there are three parts:

- Part one: *The active protagonist*
- Part two: *who struggles against primarily forces of antagonism*
- Part three: *to a closed ending of absolute irreversible change.*

McKee also said, '... regardless of background or education, everyone, consciously or instinctively, enters the story ritual with Classical anticipation. That's why this book sticks chiefly to instruction on Classical form: Beginning, Middle, End.'

# Three acts: beginning middle, end

In Dickens's *A Christmas Carol*, the three acts with their causes and effects – beginning, middle and end – are broken down as follows.

## ACT ONE

The reader meets Ebenezer Scrooge in his office on a cold Christmas Eve. The reader finds out, through the comments Scrooge makes to himself and to his overworked employee Bob Cratchit, that he hates Christmas. His characterization and his desires are revealed early in the story. Scrooge spends the evening alone, as usual, cold and miserable. He is visited by the ghost of his business partner Jacob Marley, who warns him of more ghosts to come. Marley explains that the chains that bind him are the result of the cold, bitter heart he had on earth. Marley instructs Scrooge to listen to the ghosts when they visit or an equally tormenting fate will befall him.

## ACT TWO

Act Two is similar in that there are many causes and effects, but the nature of the story means that the reader is curious to find out what the ghosts will do and say. The night begins and the first ghost, the Ghost of Christmas Past, drags Scrooge out of bed. Now, Ebenezer Scrooge's unwilling adventure begins. Scrooge is shown his life as a young man and how he had opportunities to love and be loved but turned them down. The next ghost, the Ghost of Christmas Present, reveals to Scrooge the true condition of the Cratchit family and their invalid son, Tiny Tim, and the other people in Scrooge's circle he is choosing to ignore. The third ghost, the Ghost of Christmas Yet to Come, raises the stakes and increases the tension. He reveals the sad end of Scrooge and Tiny Tim and how the future depends on the choices that Scrooge makes today.

Scrooge is left with two mutually exclusive desires: he desires to be back in his lonely, dark house doing what he always did, living selfishly, and he also desires to repent of his faults and become generous and kind, to be a part of a community and to enjoy life.

## ACT THREE

Scrooge makes his choice. He chooses life and joy over loneliness and death. He gives generously to the Cratchit family and joins his nephew for Christmas dinner. He has made a permanent, logical and feasible choice and the people around him are changed by it.

# Categorize the events in your story

Write down all the events that will take place in your story, and then put them into one of three columns, beginning, middle and end. Be as thorough as you can. One way to do this is to write specific events on index cards or use any of the apps mentioned in Chapter 3 and then you can move them around.

Now look at the three groups, things that happen in the beginning, the middle and the end. Do you see a natural separation between these events?

# Causes and effects

Take each event in your story and think about its causes. You could write the causes on the back of the index cards. What requirements must there be for this event to take place? For example, you want your main character to hold up a liquor store. What would cause him to want to do that? Is it that he's desperate for money? What would cause this desperation?

Once the causes are considered, think about the effects of the events. Your main character decides to hold up a liquor store, but finds himself in the middle of another hold-up. This changes his behaviour from criminal to heroic. Write down any effects that might result from the causes. The more you write down, the less predictable your story will be.

# Workshop

Arrange the events of each separate act in your story in chronological order. Do you see any gaps? For example, you may have your main character saving the life of the liquor-store owner in the hold-up. You may also have the main character falling in love with the store owner's daughter. The gap would be how they met and how they react to each other.

If you have gaps like this, create other events that fill that gap. For example, the store owner invites the main character over for dinner. The daughter is impressed by the heroic story, etc.

- Once you have listed all the events in chronological order, separate them by act, so that you have a beginning, a middle and an end section.
- Within each act or section, you need to decide what must come first, second and so on. This is your outline.

File this; it will be one of the most important documents you have created so far.

## Where to next?

*The next chapter goes into more detail about the requirements of the first act of the three-act structure: the 'hook', establishing setting and characters, describing their conflicts and desires, and finally the critical point of action.*

# 13

## The requirements of the first act

What are the necessary elements of a first act? The first thing is the hook, which is what grabs the attention of the reader. Then you need to establish the setting and introduce the characters, describing their actions, their immediate problems and their relationship to one another. Then you must show the most important desires of the main character, the choices he must make and the conflicts he faces. Finally, you must reveal the critical point of action – the *cause* that starts everything going.

This chapter examines in detail the first act of the classical three-act structure with reference to John Steinbeck's novella *Of Mice and Men*. To fully understand the sections, please read the book first. It is short and can be read in just a few sittings. Your local library probably has a copy and it's also available in various formats online.

John Steinbeck, *Of Mice and Men*

*'We could live offa the fatta the lan'.'*

In the opening sequence in the first act of *Of Mice and Men*, George and Lennie, migrant farm labourers, have left one disastrous job situation and are walking towards another. George introduces the reader to his big dream. Some day he and Lennie will have a place of their own. They would have crops to raise and livestock to care for. And with the mention of the animals, Lennie gets excited. He is obsessed with the idea of rabbits. Through his own dialogue, he reveals mental slowness. It's also revealed to the reader that it was Lennie's fondness for touching soft objects, such as the mouse in his pocket, that caused them to be fired from their former position.

The dialogue also communicates that the leader here is George. Lennie, despite his brute strength, is the follower. George and Lennie also argue. Caring for Lennie is a huge burden for George, but he does it for love and companionship. George says that Lennie will need to behave himself or there will be no job and no place of their own.

The first act ends as they approach the ranch to take the new job. George accepts the mission: he is to care for Lennie and keep a regular job at this new ranch.

## The elements of the first act

*Of Mice and Men* follows classical story structure. In the first act, author John Steinbeck sculpts the necessary elements for a first act so that, by the time it is over and George sets out to take the new job, the reader understands everything he needs to know to follow him and see what will happen. The first act of *Of Mice and Men* is a precise, economical beginning.

The following list contains all the important elements of a first act in the order that they should occur, so you can sculpt your own story around them. *Of Mice and Men* does all of these things.

## 1 THE HOOK

The first thing to include is the 'hook', which is whatever will immediately grab the attention of the reader. Steinbeck chose to go with a description of the scenery. It seems benign, but I think he was underscoring this part of the story because it is here where George makes his final decision.

## 2 THE SETTING

Next, without too much detail, the reader must understand the story's precise place and time. Steinbeck does this by describing Soledad, California, in the 1930s, detailing the brook, the trees and the grass where George and Lennie stop. The setting in *Of Mice and Men* could have been nowhere else but California during the Great Depression, when even able-bodied men like Lennie and George were searching for work. This desperation is an important force for both of them. Also, George gives instructions to Lennie: if there's trouble, come to this creek and I'll meet you. The setting plays a role in the story and will be revisited in the third act.

## 3 THE CHARACTERS

Then the characters are introduced to the reader. This must be done delicately, describing their actions, the problems they face and their relationship to each other. This can be done through dialogue or description. Steinbeck minimized exposition and backstory: he revealed everything he needed to reveal to the reader through dialogue. The entire dynamic of the two main characters is established through this conversation. The flaws of both – George's impatience and inner conflict in caring for Lennie and Lennie's attraction to soft, weaker things – are mentioned. Both of these weaknesses are critical to the trajectory of the plot. Notice that Steinbeck never tells the reader their life stories, how they met, why they're together or what exactly happened at the previous job. None of that information has any bearing on the plot, and the omission of that background creates a simpler, cleaner, and clearer story.

## 4 DESIRES, CHOICES AND CONFLICTS

The most important desires of the main character must be revealed. This revelation to the reader can be obvious or subtle. It can be mentioned by another character or come from the protagonist himself. Steinbeck also handles this with delicacy. As George and Lennie stop to rest, the much-loved story of their future home is repeated, mostly to amuse Lennie, but also to reveal a great deal of information to the reader.

The protagonist must make choices, either big or small, that propel him towards acceptance of his big mission. The choice the pair has made is to try out another ranch. George has also made a choice – to be faithful to Lennie regardless of his mental ability and bad habits. George enters the story conflicted. He is the main character and the reader gravitates towards him for his compassion toward Lennie, his hard luck and his willingness to work hard.

## 5 THE CRITICAL POINT OF ACTION

The critical point of action is the most important element of the first act – the *cause* that starts the action of the rest of the story. The critical point of action is never written in the first page, possibly not even in the first chapter, but is usually revealed to the reader in the first quarter of the book. At this point, the main character will make a decision – whether to accept the mission, adventure or relationship – and this decision is revealed to the reader. The supporting characters react to it. The novelist's job is to make this mission so intriguing or interesting that there will be no choice but for the reader to follow.

In *Of Mice and Men*, George is the one making the decision in this story. He decides to take another job at the next ranch with Lennie at his side, even though this may be risky. George also decides to continue telling the 'dream house' story to Lennie, even though he knows the reality of the situation. While Steinbeck doesn't make this obvious, George is a conflicted man. What propels the reader forward is curiosity about how George will handle Lennie.

The story is launched: the protagonist, George, sets off on his mission. This is the end of the first act.

Here are some further examples of critical points of action:

- Katniss Everdeen's critical point of action is the moment when she substitutes herself for her sister in the Reaping.

- Scarlett O'Hara's is when she agrees to marry Charles Hamilton and permanently devote herself to Melanie for the sake of getting closer to Ashley.
- Frodo Baggins's is when he and Sam leave the Shire with Merry and Pippin to meet Gandalf at The Prancing Pony.
- Emma Woodhouse's is when she attaches herself to Harriet Smith in order to manipulate the romance between Harriet and Mr Elton.
- Lucy Pevensie's is when she and her brothers and sisters step through the wardrobe for the first time.
- Wilbur's is when he agrees to let Charlotte save his life on the Zuckerman farm.

## Workshop

Take all your notes or index cards from the previous workshop. Examine the cards from the 'Beginning' pile only. Analyse them for the elements of a first act:

1 An opening event
2 A description of setting
3 Introduction of important characters
4 Understanding of the relationship between the characters
5 The desires, motivations or needs of the main characters
6 The critical point of action that forces the main character to embark on the journey that will be the rest of the story.

If anything is missing, free write or brainstorm about how the missing pieces could be added.

## Where to next?

*In the next chapter you will learn how to increase the tension and conflict in the second act so that the readers remain fully engaged with the protagonist and the choice he has to make.*

# 14

## The requirements of the second act

The hallmarks of the second act include rising tension; each sequence and scene is more difficult than the one before. The supporting characters show their perspectives on what the main character is doing. The antagonist also ramps up the conflict in hindering the main character. Act Two is similar to Act One in that there are many causes and effects, but the reader should now be thoroughly immersed in the protagonist's dilemma and curious to find out what the characters will do and say next. The stakes are raised and everything seems to depend on the choice that the protagonist will make between his two mutually exclusive desires.

As you learn what second acts require, you can organize your story with the same rising tension and increasing conflict.

# Increasing conflict

The second act of *Of Mice and Men* is the meat of the story. George and Lennie are engrossed in the day-to-day expectations of their new job. They quickly realize who they can trust and who they can't. Their main objectives stay the same: they still want to make money now and, naturally, stay out of trouble, so that they can buy their dream land some day. George's additional desire is to keep Lennie from repeating the mistakes of the past.

But in the second act, the increasing tension between them and the other workers makes this difficult. Their biggest antagonists are Curley and his wife. Curley is paranoid and defensive and his wife gives him reason to be. Curley and his wife have a great deal of power over the other workers and they use this power to get what they want. Each scene demonstrates this power in one way or another. George recognizes what Lennie doesn't: that this is a potentially explosive situation. Perhaps they should leave this ranch while they can. Other ranch workers see this too, and once they hear of George and Lennie's big plan to have a home of their own, they offer to help. They'll all pitch in and buy a place together. What has been just a fairy tale for Lennie's benefit could actually be a reality for George.

It looks as if there could be a happy ending for our two main characters. But then Lennie – in his strength and fascination with soft things – commits a violent act against Curley's wife, one that George has feared all along would happen. Now George is faced with choosing only one of his two mutually exclusive needs. Does he continue to defend and protect Lennie or does he keep this job and the companionship of the other men? He can't have both.

# The elements of the second act

The following list contains all the important elements of the second act that you should include in your novel.

## 1 PURSUIT OF THE GOAL

Scenes and sequences should have all the characters working either as an ensemble or as spokes in a wheel, to either help or hinder the main character in pursuit of their goal or goals. In *Of Mice and*

*Men*, the advice and warnings of the other ranch hands, in their desire to join George and Lennie in their goals, is a help for George. It makes his dreams more real and pushes him toward his ultimate desire. Then Lennie ruins everything.

## 2 DECISIONS

Circumstances force the main character to make decisions. By observing the behaviour of Curley's wife, George decides to avoid her and Curley as much as possible. He gives instructions to Lennie to do the same. But this antagonizes them more. George makes increasingly important decisions: to avoid Curley, to avoid Curley's wife, to ally himself with Candy, to lower his guard in protecting Lennie and to respond to Lennie's big mistake.

## 3 RAISING THE STAKES

Causes and events must turn the fire up under the main character. The behaviour of the other ranch hands increases George's desire to either seek their acceptance or avoid them even more. The reality of George and Lennie's dream coming true raises the stakes for their future. The response to Lennie's violence causes George to orchestrate a cover-up, buy some time and give Lennie instructions to meet at the hiding spot they found in the first act.

## 4 FALSE HOPES, BETRAYAL OR SECRETS REVEALED

A false hope or two, a betrayal or a secret revealed makes the main character react in a way that is especially challenging. The false hope for George is when Candy suggests that they pool their resources to buy a house. For just a moment, he believes that this will be the answer to all of his and Lennie's problems.

## 5 ACTION AND DIALOGUE

Plenty of action and dialogue in each of the scenes and sequences should propel the main character towards the goal. In *Of Mice and Men*, none of the ranch hands is actually seen working. Instead they are resting, playing games, having conversations and avoiding getting into trouble. There's plenty of conflict and not only are the characters' inner lives and desires revealed in the dialogue, but the dialogue is the vehicle that propels the plot forward.

## 6 GROWING TENSION

The tension must grow with each scene, sequence and chapter. Each beat builds on the one before. In *Of Mice and Men,* the reader should be teased – will George and Lennie make it to their dream home? Will they fail miserably? Back and forth, this hope and hopelessness should both be seen until the final scenes when the choice is made.

## 7 THE CHOICE

As the conflict increases, with each sequence and scene more tense than the one before, the supporting characters respond to what the main character is doing. The antagonist also increases the conflict in hindering the main character. Steinbeck crafts all of this beautifully, right up to George's decision. The reader really doesn't know what choice George is going to make.

## Write about the choice

In your notes, make sure that there is a false hope, a secret betrayed or a fear realized. Do a free write on how this will propel your protagonist to the position of making the choice between his mutually exclusive needs.

Here are some further examples of second-act choice making:

- Katniss Everdeen's second-act choice comes when she and Peeta are sitting on the Cornucopia and one of them has to kill the other.
- Emma Woodhouse's occurs when, after all her matchmaking attempts made on Harriet's behalf, Harriet announces that it is really Mr Knightly she is attracted to. Emma is also conflicted over the way she has treated Miss Bates. Emma's place in her society's circle is now unstable.

- Lucy Pevensie's starts when she, Edmund, Peter and Susan decide to follow Mr and Mrs Beaver and it concludes at Stone Table where Lucy and Susan witness Aslan's death. They have to choose whether or not to follow Aslan's instructions.

## Workshop

Review all your notes and index cards for Act Two.

1 If you haven't already, arrange the scenes and sequences in order from least tense to most tense. The most tense of all should put your protagonist in a position where he has to make a choice between two mutually exclusive needs.

2 Review the roles of the supporting characters. Examine how they are helping or hindering the protagonist in his goals. Review what their individual desires are in contrast to what the protagonist wants. Make notes of how they can pursue their goals in this act.

3 What causes do you have in Act Two? Have you come up with believable yet interesting effects for them? If you're having trouble, work backwards. Start with the choice your protagonist makes. What happens immediately before? And before that? List what happens to him to put him in that position. These are the effects. What are the causes?

## Where to next?

*The next chapter covers all the elements of the third act, when you will decide on the choices your main character will make that will create a satisfying ending to your story.*

# 15

## The requirements of the third act

In classic story structure, the third act is when the mess is cleaned up. Sometimes there's a learning moment. There may even be a 'We'd have got away with it too if it hadn't been for these meddling kids' type of ending. The third act should be complete enough that readers understand the conclusions, see the logic and necessity of it and savour the resonance with satisfaction. Emma and Mr Knightley get engaged! Aslan rules Narnia and the White Witch is dead! Katniss and Peeta are local heroes and start a revolution! Or it may be an ending like Scarlett's, where she is left alone in her huge house, having pushed away everyone who matters to her.

Happy or sad, the third-act ending has to have a sense of permanence. As you read this chapter, think what permanent decisions you want your main character to make.

*Lennie said, 'I thought you was mad at me, George.' 'No,'*
*said George. 'No, Lennie. I ain't mad. I never been mad,*
*an' I ain't now. That's a thing I want ya to know.' The*
*voices came close now. George raised the gun and listened*
*to the voices. Lennie begged, 'Le's do it now. Le's get that*
*place now.' 'Sure, right now. I gotta. We gotta.'*
John Steinbeck, *Of Mice and Men* (1937)

The third act of *Of Mice and Men* occurs when George gives Lennie instructions to leave the ranch and return to the site of Act One. George meets him there and has already decided what the next step will be. George's next actions move quickly and permanently. George's tragic choice changes the lives of everyone in the story.

This is the moment that the readers have been waiting for. It is in this final moment that the questions have all been answered. It is impossible for the characters to return to who they were in Act One.

# The elements of the third act

The following list contains all the important elements of the third act that you should include.

## 1 A TYING UP OF LOOSE ENDS

Every detail mentioned casually in the first act will have a purpose here. You don't go on and on about someone's sword collection in the third chapter if you're not going to use one of those swords to battle the assailant later.

## 2 A SATISFYING ENDING

All characters have given their all to the story, one way or another. The ending is permanent and inevitable.

## 3 RESONANCE

Hints of values or morals or themes should swell up in this section like a crescendo. Ideally, the reader fully sees why the writer made the choices that they made. When a reader comes away from the book, they will be reminded of a universal truth or a significant value and they will see, hopefully not too heavy-handedly, that there is something to learn in this story.

## Focus point

By the end of a novel, the satisfied reader should take a deep sigh and say, 'Oh!' By this point you want your reader to have understood the nuances and foreshadowing and symbolism that you have included throughout your story more completely.

## Workshop

Do this exercise in three ten-minute increments, one for each stage.

- Review all your notes and index cards for Act Three. Then review all the notes from Acts One and Two and look for loose ends that will need tying up.
- Make notes on how every character will respond to the permanent choice that the main character makes. Do they need to express themselves in the third act?
- Consider what emotions you want your reader to leave with when they close the book. Make notes on how this can be instilled in the third act.

## Where to next?

*In the next chapter we will look at the more detailed framework of your story, examining how each act is broken down into the sequences, scenes and beats that push your narrative along.*

# 16

## Sequences, scenes and beats

This chapter is about understanding the more detailed framework of your story. As we have seen, the biggest units are the three acts, each of which has a specific purpose that must be fulfilled. Within each act are sequences, within the sequences are scenes, and within the scenes are beats.

Each act is a group of sequences that form the story into major critical points of action for the main character. Each sequence is a group of scenes that move the story within the act. Scenes have the single purpose of progressing the story within the sequence. Each beat in a scene is a short interchange or event that pushes or pulls the main character into a rising emotional journey for the sake of accomplishing their ultimate goal. Each scene has a series of these beats.

# Your story framework

## Louis L'Amour

*'One day I was speeding along at the typewriter, and my daughter – who was a child at the time – asked me, "Daddy, why are you writing so fast?" And I replied, "Because I want to see how the story turns out!"'*

As you get closer to the drafting stage of story sculpting, you will need to understand how to build a framework that comprises sequences, scenes and beats and how they combine to make an act. The term 'chapter' is not a term needed in this analysis because it is just an arbitrary container for scenes and sequences. A chapter division is fully a style choice and the author can choose how chapters are divided according to this.

The purpose of sequences and scenes is to work together, increasing the tension between the characters, bringing the protagonist along to the next event, creating causes so that the effects pull or push the protagonist to the next sequence and the next act. The beats are the points within a scene that charge the protagonist towards either a positive response or a negative one. As the beats flow, the hero is propelled further in the grand mission or else is discouraged and quits.

### SCENES

It is in scenes that the essence of the story is shown. In scenes, each character is put in different situations. They have distinct gains or losses. They take steps either towards or away from their ultimate goals. It is in writing the scenes that you can be your most creative.

Each scene should have a distinct gain or loss for the main characters. What is it? If it is a loss, then you are setting up hope that perhaps the next scene will regain it. In *Gone with the Wind*, Scarlett spends a great deal of time – too much, apparently – at Aunt Pittypat's house, delivering Melanie's baby, and then she realizes that Atlanta is burning around her. Scarlett is at a loss. She's slipped down Maslow's hierarchy and now needs to survive. She's lost her city, her food source and all safety. This scene is brutal but it drives her to the next scene – the escape through Atlanta with Rhett.

This journey scene and the beats of their conversation reveal more information: Sherman is marching to the sea and the Confederate Army is now in retreat. There is little hope – so little, in fact that Rhett decides to enlist. Scarlett, shocked by this news, is all the more driven to survive. She chooses to return to Tara in the false hope that her family will be there to take responsibility off her shoulders. In each new scene, things get worse and worse for poor Scarlett. But what is her final stance in this sequence? She stands defiantly in the remains of her ruined lands, grips the earth with her worn hands and recollects her father's devotion to Tara. She has changed. 'As God is my witness, I'll never be hungry again.'

# Analysing a sequence

The following extract is a chapter taken from *Around the World in Eighty Days* (1874). This Jules Verne classic is full of adventure and shows in scene after scene how the tension builds and how Phileas Fogg and his sidekick Passepartout always get out of trouble in the nick of time. The plot of the book revolves around Phileas's desire to travel from London eastwards across Europe, Asia, the Pacific Ocean, the Americas and back to London in 80 days – a remarkable feat for the period. Fogg has scheduled his journey perfectly and so the party doesn't have time to stop and save a damsel in distress in the jungles of India. But they are gentlemen, so they have to.

In this chapter, which is also a sequence, Fogg, Passepartout and their companion Sir Francis are asking their guide, an Indian Parsee, to give them information about the woman in peril and together they are trying to save her and catch the next train on time. They form a plan and implement it, but it doesn't end as they expect.

Within the following sequence, the word SCENE is placed where a new scene takes place. Think of 'scene' as if this were a film and a new place of action was needed. A change of scene is indicated when the characters move to a new location or a period of time has passed.

The word BEAT is placed to indicate a new event, realization, piece of information or action. It is a unit of measurement for the pulse of the story. A beat is not a paragraph, but it can be contained in one. Notice how many beats make up a scene, with each scene either pushing or pulling Fogg towards or away from his desires. Notice also the 'head-hopping': this is an example of omniscient point of view. Notice also how description and exposition pepper the story. My notes are in italics.

---

**SCENE – The characters make a plan.**

BEAT

The project was a bold one, full of difficulty, perhaps impracticable. Mr Fogg was going to risk life, or at least liberty, and therefore the success of his tour. But he did not hesitate, and he found in Sir Francis Cromarty an enthusiastic ally. *Mr Phileas Fogg's mutually exclusive desires are revealed!*

As for Passepartout, he was ready for anything that might be proposed. His master's idea charmed him; he perceived a heart, a soul, under that icy exterior. He began to love Phileas Fogg. *Passepartout, the companion or 'buddy' is allying himself emotionally with the daring and mysterious Mr Fogg. This is a push towards Fogg's goals.*

BEAT

There remained the guide: what course would he adopt? Would he not take part with the Indians? In default of his assistance, it was necessary to be assured of his neutrality.

Sir Francis frankly put the question to him.

'Officers,' replied the guide, 'I am a Parsee, and this woman is a Parsee. Command me as you will.'

'Excellent!' said Mr Fogg. *The compliance of the Parsee is a push toward Fogg's goals.*

BEAT

'However,' resumed the guide, 'it is certain, not only that we shall risk our lives, but horrible tortures, if we are taken.' The stakes are raised. *This Parsee knows what will happen if they fail. This is a pull against Fogg's goals.*

'That is foreseen,' replied Mr Fogg. 'I think we must wait till night before acting.'

'I think so,' said the guide.

---

**BEAT**

The worthy Indian then gave some account of the victim, who, he said, was a celebrated beauty of the Parsee race, and the daughter of a wealthy Bombay merchant. She had received a thoroughly English education in that city, and, from her manners and intelligence, would be thought a European. Her name was Aouda. Left an orphan, she was married against her will to the old rajah of Bundelcund; and, knowing the fate that awaited her, she escaped, was retaken, and devoted by the rajah's relatives, who had an interest in her death, to the sacrifice from which it seemed she could not escape. *The stakes are raised even higher. The fair lady's life is in danger! This is a pull against Fogg's goals.*

**BEAT**

The Parsee's narrative only confirmed Mr Fogg and his companions in their generous design. It was decided that the guide should direct the elephant towards the pagoda of Pillaji, which he accordingly approached as quickly as possible. They halted, half an hour afterwards, in a copse, some five hundred feet from the pagoda, where they were well concealed; but they could hear the groans and cries of the fakirs distinctly. *This is description. It is neutral and has no value for or against Fogg's goals.*

**BEAT**

They then discussed the means of getting at the victim. The guide was familiar with the pagoda of Pillaji, in which, as he declared, the young woman was imprisoned. Could they enter any of its doors while the whole party of Indians was plunged in a drunken sleep, or was it safer to attempt to make a hole in the walls? This could only be determined at the moment and the place themselves; but it was certain that the abduction must be made that night, and not when, at break of day, the victim was led to her funeral pyre. Then no human intervention could save her. *This is exposition: also neutral.*

## SCENE – The characters implement the plan.

BEAT

As soon as night fell, about six o'clock, they decided to make a reconnaissance around the pagoda. The cries of the fakirs were just ceasing; the Indians were in the act of plunging themselves into the drunkenness caused by liquid opium mingled with hemp, and it might be possible to slip between them to the temple itself. *Everyone is stoned. This is a push toward Fogg's goals.*

The Parsee, leading the others, noiselessly crept through the wood, and in ten minutes they found themselves on the banks of a small stream, whence, by the light of the rosin torches, they perceived a pyre of wood, on the top of which lay the embalmed body of the rajah, which was to be burned with his wife. The pagoda, whose minarets loomed above the trees in the deepening dusk, stood a hundred steps away. *Description. Neutral.*

BEAT

'Come!' whispered the guide.

He slipped more cautiously than ever through the brush, followed by his companions; the silence around was only broken by the low murmuring of the wind among the branches.

Soon the Parsee stopped on the borders of the glade, which was lit up by the torches. The ground was covered by groups of the Indians, motionless in their drunken sleep; it seemed a battlefield strewn with the dead. Men, women, and children lay together. They look helpless. *This is a push toward Fogg's goals.*

In the background, among the trees, the pagoda of Pillaji loomed distinctly. Much to the guide's disappointment, the guards of the rajah, lighted by torches, were watching at the doors and marching to and fro with naked sabres; probably the priests, too, were watching within. *This is dangerous for our heroes! Their tension is increasing! This is a pull against Fogg's goals.*

BEAT

The Parsee, now convinced that it was impossible to force an entrance to the temple, advanced no farther, but led his companions back again. Phileas Fogg and Sir Francis Cromarty also saw that nothing could be attempted in that direction. They stopped, and engaged in a whispered colloquy.

'It is only eight now,' said the brigadier, 'and these guards may also go to sleep.'

'It is not impossible,' returned the Parsee.

They lay down at the foot of a tree, and waited. *This is a pull against Fogg's goals.*

**SCENE – This isn't working as they had hoped. They'll wait a bit longer and try again. But time is running out!**

BEAT

The time seemed long; the guide ever and anon left them to take an observation on the edge of the wood, but the guards watched steadily by the glare of the torches, and a dim light crept through the windows of the pagoda.

They waited till midnight; but no change took place among the guards, and it became apparent that their yielding to sleep could not be counted on. The other plan must be carried out; an opening in the walls of the pagoda must be made. It remained to ascertain whether the priests were watching by the side of their victim as assiduously as were the soldiers at the door. *This is a pull against Fogg's goals because it will take more time. He has a train to catch!*

BEAT

After a last consultation, the guide announced that he was ready for the attempt, and advanced, followed by the others. They took a roundabout way, so as to get at the pagoda on the rear. They reached the walls about half-past twelve, without having met anyone; here there was no guard, nor were there either windows or doors.

The night was dark. The moon, on the wane, scarcely left the horizon, and was covered with heavy clouds; the height of the trees deepened the darkness. *All description.*

BEAT

It was not enough to reach the walls; an opening in them must be accomplished, and to attain this purpose the party only had their pocket-knives. Happily the temple walls were built of brick and wood, which could be penetrated with little difficulty; after one brick had been taken out, the rest would yield easily. *This is a push toward Fogg's goals.*

They set noiselessly to work, and the Parsee on one side and Passepartout on the other began to loosen the bricks so as to make an aperture two feet wide. They were getting on rapidly, when suddenly a cry was heard in the interior of the temple, followed almost instantly by other cries replying from the outside. Passepartout and the guide stopped. Had they been heard? Was the alarm being given? Common prudence urged them to retire, and they did so, followed by Phileas Fogg and Sir Francis. They again hid themselves in the wood, and waited till the disturbance, whatever it might be, ceased, holding themselves ready to resume their attempt without delay. But, awkwardly enough, the guards now appeared at the rear of the temple, and there installed themselves, in readiness to prevent a surprise. *Oh no! The guards are back! This is a pull against Fogg's goals.*

It would be difficult to describe the disappointment of the party, thus interrupted in their work. They could not now reach the victim; how, then, could they save her? Sir Francis shook his fists, Passepartout was beside himself, and the guide gnashed his teeth with rage. The tranquil Fogg waited, without betraying any emotion. *Conflict! This raises the stakes! This is a pull against Fogg's goals!*

BEAT

'We have nothing to do but to go away,' whispered Sir Francis.

'Nothing but to go away,' echoed the guide.

'Stop,' said Fogg. 'I am only due at Allahabad tomorrow before noon.' *He reminds the reader of his goals.*

'But what can you hope to do?' asked Sir Francis. 'In a few hours it will be daylight, and—'

'The chance which now seems lost may present itself at the last moment.' *Hope!*

BEAT

Sir Francis would have liked to read Phileas Fogg's eyes. What was this cool Englishman thinking of? Was he planning to make a rush for the young woman at the very moment of the sacrifice, and boldly snatch her from her executioners? *These questions remind the reader of the ultimate objective of Phileas Fogg yet it also brings up the problem of a damsel in distress. These questions explain Phileas's two mutually exclusive desires again.*

This would be utter folly, and it was hard to admit that Fogg was such a fool. Sir Francis consented, however, to remain to the end of this terrible drama. The guide led them to the rear of the glade, where they were able to observe the sleeping groups.

BEAT

Meanwhile Passepartout, who had perched himself on the lower branches of a tree, was resolving an idea which had at first struck him like a flash, and which was now firmly lodged in his brain.

He had commenced by saying to himself, 'What folly!' and then he repeated, 'Why not, after all? It's a chance perhaps the only one; and with such sots!' Thinking thus, he slipped, with the suppleness of a serpent, to the lowest branches, the ends of which bent almost to the ground. *The reader is not aware of his plans. This creates tension and suspense. We have to find out what happens now!*

**SCENE – Since they have nothing else to do, they might as well wait until daybreak.**

BEAT

The hours passed, and the lighter shades now announced the approach of day, though it was not yet light. This was the moment. The slumbering multitude became animated, the tambourines sounded, songs and cries arose; the hour of the sacrifice had come. The doors of the pagoda swung open, and a bright light escaped from its interior, in the midst of which Mr Fogg and Sir Francis espied the victim. She seemed, having shaken off the stupor of intoxication, to be striving to escape from her executioner. Sir Francis's heart throbbed; and, convulsively seizing Mr Fogg's hand, found in it an open knife. Just at this moment the crowd began to move. The young woman had again fallen into a stupor caused by the fumes of hemp, and passed among the fakirs, who escorted her with their wild, religious cries. *It's time for our heroes to take action!*

BEAT

Phileas Fogg and his companions, mingling in the rear ranks of the crowd, followed; and in two minutes they reached the banks of the stream, and stopped fifty paces from the pyre, upon which still lay the rajah's corpse. In the semi-obscurity they saw the victim, quite senseless, stretched out beside her husband's body. Then a torch was brought, and the wood, heavily soaked with oil, instantly took fire.

BEAT

At this moment Sir Francis and the guide seized Phileas Fogg, who, in an instant of mad generosity, was about to rush upon the pyre. But he had quickly pushed them aside, when the whole scene suddenly changed. A cry of terror arose. The whole multitude prostrated themselves, terror-stricken, on the ground.

The old rajah was not dead, then, since he rose of a sudden, like a spectre, took up his wife in his arms, and descended from the pyre in the midst of the clouds of smoke, which only heightened his ghostly appearance. *The unexpected has happened! A dead man has risen!*

Fakirs and soldiers and priests, seized with instant terror, lay there, with their faces on the ground, not daring to lift their eyes and behold such a prodigy.

The inanimate victim was borne along by the vigorous arms which supported her, and which she did not seem in the least to burden. Mr Fogg and Sir Francis stood erect, the Parsee bowed his head, and Passepartout was, no doubt, scarcely less stupefied.

The resuscitated rajah approached Sir Francis and Mr Fogg, and, in an abrupt tone, said, 'Let us be off!' *What just happened? Can Fogg attain both of his mutually exclusive desires?*

BEAT

It was Passepartout himself, who had slipped upon the pyre in the midst of the smoke and, profiting by the still overhanging darkness, had delivered the young woman from death! It was Passepartout who, playing his part with a happy audacity, had passed through the crowd amid the general terror. *Passepartout unexpectedly becomes the hero, not Fogg. This endears him to the reader and creates a bond between the two characters.*

### SCENE – Passepartout proves to be a clever sidekick! Now to make that train!

BEAT

A moment after all four of the party had disappeared in the woods, and the elephant was bearing them away at a rapid pace. But the cries and noise, and a ball which whizzed through Phileas Fogg's hat, apprised them that the trick had been discovered.

The old rajah's body, indeed, now appeared upon the burning pyre; and the priests, recovered from their terror, perceived that an abduction had taken place. They hastened into the forest, followed by the soldiers, who fired a volley after the fugitives; but the latter rapidly increased the distance between them, and ere long found themselves beyond the reach of the bullets and arrows. *Happy ever after. Now, on to the next chapter where even more close calls are in store for Phileas Fogg and Passepartout.*

(From Jules Verne, *Around the World in Eighty Days*, trans. George Makepeace Towle, 1874)

## Recognizing scenes and beats

Read a chapter from a favourite novel, one you are intimately familiar with. Try to recognize scenes and beats. Notice whether the action and dialogue push or pull the protagonist towards or away from his goals.

## Draft a sequence

Write a sequence from your work in progress, one that's at least two double-spaced pages long. It doesn't have to be perfect, just written. During the drafting of this scene, try not to think about anything but the story. Then, when you have finished, go back and mark where the scenes changed and where the beats were. Note any description or backstory you wrote. Then mark where the pushes and pulls were for your antagonist. Did you increase your tension? Did you have any fresh insight?

## Where to next?

*You should now have a plot, a setting, characters with goals and desires, a narrative voice and a three-act structure. The next chapter covers another vital element of your story: the dialogue.*

# 17

## Dialogue

Good dialogue takes a story from being a narrative to being real. It gives the reader a chance to be a fly on the wall in every scene. Good dialogue is easy to read and your readers will enjoy reading it. It can be as action packed as a chase scene or as still as a dream. Good dialogue can illuminate conflict and keep the story moving at a good pace. Good dialogue can set the tone of the story, enhance character, and provide exposition. It can build tension, be a great place for humour, and it can be fun to write.

This chapter describes how to create good dialogue and explains the mistakes that many authors make in writing it.

*Mr. Darcy stood near them in silent indignation at such a mode of passing the evening, to the exclusion of all conversation, and was too much engrossed by his thoughts to perceive that Sir William Lucas was his neighbour, till Sir William thus began:*

*'What a charming amusement for young people this is, Mr. Darcy! There is nothing like dancing after all. I consider it as one of the first refinements of polished society.'*

*'Certainly, sir; and it has the advantage also of being in vogue amongst the less polished societies of the world. Every savage can dance.'*

**Jane Austen,** *Pride and Prejudice* **(1813)**

*'But I don't want to go among mad people,' Alice remarked.*

*'Oh, you can't help that,' said the Cat: 'we're all mad here. I'm mad. You're mad.'*

*'How do you know I'm mad?' said Alice.*

*'You must be,' said the Cat, or you wouldn't have come here.'*

**Lewis Carroll,** *Alice's Adventures in Wonderland* **(1865)**

*'Well, does it make sense to you?'*

*He said, 'It doesn't have to, it's something that happens. It's like seeing a person you never saw before – you could be passing on the street – and you look at each other ...'*

*Karen was nodding. 'You make eye contact without meaning to.'*

*'And for a few moments,' Foley said, 'there's a kind of recognition. You look at each other and you know something.'*

*'That no one else knows,' Karen said. 'You see it in their eyes.'*

*'And the next moment the person's gone,' Foley said, 'and it's too late to do anything*

*about it, but you remember it because it*
*was right there and you let it go, and you think,*
*What if I had stopped and said something?*
*It might happen only a few times in your life.'*
'Or once,' Karen said.

Elmore Leonard, *Out of Sight* (William Morrow, 1996)

'Good afternoon,' he said. 'I see
*you all had you a little spill.'*
*'We turned over twice!' said the grandmother.*
*'Oncet,' he corrected. 'We seen it happen.*
*Try their car and see will it run, Hiram,'*
*he said quietly to the boy with the*
*gay hat.*
*'What you got that gun for?' John*
*Wesley asked. 'Whatcha gonna do with that gun?'*
*'Lady,' the man said to the children's mother, 'would you*
*mind calling them children to sit down by you? Children*
*make me nervous. I want all you all to sit down right*
*together there where you're at.'*
*'What are you telling US what to do for?' June Star asked.*
*Behind them the line of woods gaped like dark open*
*mouth. 'Come here, 'said their mother.*
*'Look here now,' Bailey began suddenly, 'we're in a*
*predicament! We're in ...'*
*The grandmother shrieked. She scrambled*
*to her feet and stood staring. 'You're the*
*Misfit!' she said. 'I recognized you at once!'*

Flannery O'Connor, 'A Good Man Is Hard to Find', in *A Good
Man Is Hard to Find* (Harcourt, Brace & Co., 1955)

This book has used the sculpture metaphor to describe the elements
of the story-creating process, but something is still missing: the soul.
Sometimes, if you look at a classical Greek or Roman sculpture, you
can recognize its inner humanity. It has vibrancy and movement, and
seems almost to be alive, even though it is forever still in marble.

In fiction, readers can experience this same feeling, this sense of the animation and energy, through the dialogue.

Sloppy, lazy dialogue can be a problem and it can take away from the liveliness of the story. Dialogue that is too laden with dialects, phonetic spellings, colloquialisms or slang can be off-putting. Dialogue with long sentences is unrealistic and unnatural. Dialogue that includes chitchat, small talk or asks what the characters did over the weekend drags down the pace and puts the reader to sleep. Dialogue that isn't carefully sculpted with precise word choice, the right dialogue tags, blocking and with regard to pacing can weaken a story. Dialogue that is too heavy on exposition can be annoying: 'As you know, Mabel, my husband left me for another woman and I went through a nasty divorce.'

Like every other part of this story that you are writing, your dialogue must be believable, engaging and concise. It must move the story forward. Dialogue is the life of the story. Take time to make it real.

# How to write good dialogue

The first thing you need to do in order to write good dialogue is understand your characters. Understand what they want, what their big secrets are – and their big lies. Have a precise idea of how they talk. Understand their relationship to everyone else and what they think of everyone else in the story. Put words in their mouths. Free write their thoughts and what they say to themselves about this story, and what not just the main character but also the other characters say about their objectives.

There are three further things you need to do to develop your skill in writing dialogue:

1 Study dialogue constantly. Listen carefully to dialogue in television shows, which is written economically. Also pay attention to the way others speak around you. Do they have bad habits, interrupt, use 'um' or 'uh' too frequently?

2 Practise writing dialogue. Your skill with dialogue will be a huge indicator to an agent or publisher of your strength as a storyteller.

3 Read. Reading is your creative fuel. Pay attention to the way other authors write their dialogue and learn from them.

# MAKING YOUR DIALOGUE AUTHENTIC

You must be able to write dialogue that is believable and just as full of life as your characters.

Your dialogue has to be a pared-down example of what would really happen if two people were talking together. In real life, two people would be interrupted. One would have attention issues or be naturally indecisive. He may not be able to respond to the requests of the other quickly. One would be a fast talker and a fast thinker and demand that their partner speak faster. The mundane details of the day would be mentioned. One of them would use 'um' and 'so' and 'uh' all the time. If you dictated exactly what you heard two people talk about, you might well be disappointed in how dull it is.

But there are plenty of things you can add to make your dialogue more authentic:

- **Find conflict.**
  Your characters should *not* get along. They should find trivial things to disagree about. They should be annoyed with the mess left on the kitchen counter. They should wonder where everybody's been. Real people do this, so if your characters do it, it will feel real to your reader. Make a list of all the ways your characters can be in conflict with one another that have nothing to do with the plot.

- **Stay short.**
  Rarely do people make long speeches unless, of course, they are behind a pulpit, standing in front of a class, making a toast or have been just given an important award. Keep your exchanges between your characters short and to the point. Real people talk this way, so your characters should too.

- **Keep secrets.**
  Generally speaking, real people hide their vulnerabilities. Real people don't open up about their heartache or their love life or their plans for the bank heist unless they are in a safe, isolated space. They also don't tell the complete truth. Keep this in mind if you don't want your characters' secrets to be revealed. If you put your character in an awkward place and have him be reluctant to share his secret, this will add to your conflict. This is what you want.

- **Speak rhetorically.**
  People often talk to hear themselves talk without expecting an answer. If done sparingly, you could let your characters speak rhetorically to avoid giving information or being annoying. Consider using this in your dialogue. It will add to its authenticity.

- **Rarely address your characters by name.**
  In everyday language, people rarely say names out loud, unless it is in greeting or to give instruction or to get attention. Real people don't say, 'Chris, it's obvious who the murderer is.' They would just say, 'It's obvious who the murderer is.' Overusing people's names in dialogue looks amateurish. Cut back on using names, unless the name adds to the meaning of what is said.

- **Use bad grammar and incomplete sentences.**
  One of the fun parts of writing dialogue is not worrying too much about precise grammar. In real life, people speak in fragments, so you can do this with your dialogue. You can also use colloquialisms sparingly – as long as the meaning doesn't suffer and the reader doesn't struggle to understand it: 'Nope. That's not gonna work. I think we should take the truck into the shop and see if we can replace that gauge. George ain't gonna like it. But I don't care.'

## MAKING YOUR DIALOGUE ACTION-PACKED

Just as a scene has beats that push and pull the desires of the characters along, dialogue can do the same thing. The characterization, blocking and pace of the characters as they speak create beats and either decrease or increase the pulse of the story and what is happening. Skilled writers can make the most boring of scenes feel more alive with a few additions.

The following is an example of dialogue between two law enforcement officers looking at a computer screen: a scene that is potentially boring. This is hardly Pulitzer Prize-winning dialogue, but it is similar to what you might view on a crime drama television show. I chose this because scenes like this are common and writers have to work hard to make them interesting.

This is the version with the words only. What can you learn from the characters? What's their desire?

'Do you think he's trying to pull one over on us?'

'Maybe. See how he left these footprints here. See how he dodged the security camera at the corner? And we know he headed south on foot a few minutes later.'

'South towards the river!'

'Exactly. He was five minutes away from the Jerrigan crime scene!'

'I'll tell the chief. He'll want to gather the squadron and ambush him from the Johnston Bridge.'

'No, tell the chief we know where he is, but that's all. The Johnston Bridge could be the worst place to be tonight. It could be a distraction from the real problem. The civic centre is their real target.'

'How do you know?'

'I have a hunch.'

If this were a scene on television, it would be up to the actors to fill in the rest of the information, like characterization and desires. But if this scene were in a novel, then the writer would need to enhance the characters. He would need to choose vibrant words and pay attention to sentence length. He would need precise dialogue tags and he would need to block what the characters are doing.

In the previous exchange, the two characters are flat, practically archetypal. They have no names, no basic description, no characterization and certainly no desires. In the following rewrite of the dialogue, I've added more dimensions to who they are, but only in the actual words they say. Read it and see whether you can get a better picture of the two speakers. The investigator is now Hank and the co-worker is Rawley.

Rawley: 'I hate smart perps. I hate it that they think they can pull one over on us. Is that what this guy is trying to do?'

Hank: 'Maybe. See? Footprints. He dodged the security camera at the corner. Then he headed south. On foot.'

Rawley: 'South towards the river! This guys's smart! Dude!'

Hank: 'Exactly. Five minutes away from the Jerrigan crime scene.'

Rawley: 'I'll tell the chief. He'll want to gather the squadron. We could ambush him from the Johnston Bridge!'

Hank: 'No. Don't tell the chief that. The Johnston Bridge could be the worst place to be tonight. It's a distraction from the real problem. The civic centre is their target.'

Rawley: 'What? No way. The civic centre? But how would? No, he couldn't. How do you know?'

Hank: 'I have a hunch.'

Besides giving the characters' names, I also tinkered with Hank's sentence length. Shorter sentences are like staccato notes – precise and clear. Hank doesn't reveal any more information than he has to. Hank is all business. I also gave Rawley a lot of emotional responses to Hank's information. He's a bit impulsive and annoying. He has short sentences too, but his sentences are short because he gets distracted easily and argues with himself in his dialogue. He also uses more interjections because he's emotional.

The revised version gives a clearer picture of the two characters. The word choices and sentence length enhance their character without taking away from the story. But I can add even more. This time, the exchange has their names removed and dialogue tags added in. Dialogue tags can also enhance the characters and give more information to the reader.

## ADDING DIALOGUE TAGS

You've been aware of dialogue tags, such as *said, spoke, whispered, yelled, mumbled, muttered, cried, agreed* and *bellowed,* since you were a child. (There are hundreds more in a thesaurus.) I'd like to argue that dialogue tags should be used as a chef uses seasoning in a dish: sparingly, and only to enhance the dialogue and never to draw attention to themselves.

'I hate smart perps,' Rawley whined. 'I hate it that they think they can pull one over on us. Is that what this guy is trying to do?'

'Maybe. See? Footprints. He dodged the security camera at the corner. Then he headed south. On foot,' Hank said.

Rawley yelled. 'South towards the river! This guys's smart! Dude!'

'Exactly,' Hank muttered. 'Five minutes away from the Jerrigan crime scene.'

'I'll tell the chief. He'll want to gather the squadron. We could ambush him from the Johnston Bridge!' Rawley said.

'No,' Hank interrupted. 'Don't tell the chief that. The Johnston Bridge could be the worst place to be tonight. It's a distraction from the real problem. The civic centre is their target.'

'What? No way. The civic centre? But how would? No, he couldn't. How do you know?'

'I have a hunch,' Hank said.

The dialogue tags used in this exchange are *whined, said, yelled, muttered, said, interrupted* and *said* again. *Whined* and *yelled* are attributed to Rawley and a reader could infer that he is passionate and emotional. *Muttered* is given to Hank, which tells the reader that he is less emotional, but then he *interrupted,* which indicates that he has a new thought he decides is important. The verb *said* gives no additional information, nor does it enhance the dialogue. One line has no tag at all. It wasn't needed because reader could infer who was speaking.

## BLOCKING AND PACING

Blocking is a theatre term that describes the action that an actor will take, either with his body or his hands, while he is speaking. Pacing is the way you can speed up or slow down the action. The next changes to the dialogue address blocking and pacing.

Rawley bounded up behind Hank. 'I hate smart perps. I hate it that they think they can pull one over on us. Is that what this guy is trying to do?'

Hank took a deep breath. He looked at the footage on his computer. 'Maybe. See? Footprints.' Hank pointed to the screen and squinted. 'He dodged the security camera at the corner. Then he headed south. On foot.'

Rawley gasped. 'South towards the river! This guy's smart. Dude!'

Hank looked at Rawley for the first time. 'Exactly. Five minutes away from the Jerrigan crime scene.'

Rawley fumbled with his cellphone. 'I'll tell the chief. He'll want to gather the squadron. We could ambush him from the Johnston Bridge!'

'No,' Hank touched his arm. 'Don't tell the chief that. The Johnston Bridge could be the worst place to be tonight.' Hank shook his head and looked back at the screen. 'It's a distraction from the real problem.' He swallowed. 'The civic centre is their target.'

Rawley dropped his phone. 'What? No way. The civic centre? But how would? No, he couldn't. How do you know?'

Hank nodded his head. 'I have a hunch.'

Novelists should consider blocking while they sculpt dialogue because action is more effective than dialogue tags in adding to the emotion of the scene:

- 'I hate smart perps,' Rawley whined.
- Rawley bounded up behind Hank. 'I hate smart perps.'

Of these two sentences, the second one creates a more vivid picture of what Rawley is doing. Thoughtful blocking can be a good substitute for weak dialogue tags.

Also notice the pacing of this scene: how the placement of the blocking speeds up or slows down the dialogue between Rawley and Hank. Rawley is impulsive and energetic. This is shown through the way he acts before thinking, bounds up to Hank's desk and fumbles with his phone. He jumps to conclusions and wants to take action. Hank, on the other hand, is slower and more thoughtful. I show this in the way he never looks at Rawley until the end, how he rarely moves his body and how he appears to be mulling something over.

## Watch television

Pick a thriller, detective or crime show in which a lot of information is spoken between the characters. Note how many times information is exchanged. Also note how few times characters chitchat, how they never talk about their families or the weather. Note how few times they say 'er' or 'um' or stumble over their words as real people do.

## Write some dialogue

Write a dialogue between your protagonist and your sceptic, in which the main character has decided to go on his big quest, but the sceptic opposes it. The main character knows how the sceptic feels but tries to convince him anyway. Your dialogue will be about the conversation with both characters making their points. Don't put in any stage direction or movement for the characters; just write down their words.

## Rewrite the dialogue

Take this same dialogue and rewrite it. This time, change the sceptic just slightly. In this version, the protagonist has no idea that the sceptic opposes his plan. Think about how your sceptic can evade the protagonist's questions, try to change the subject and ask pointed questions. Your sceptic is trying to persuade the protagonist to discard the plan but doesn't want to be seen as unsupportive. How does this change or enhance the characters and the story?

## Edit the scene

Review the scene you wrote and look for long sentences. Omit chitchat and gratuitous exposition. Make sure that your word choices are clear and specific, and that your dialogue tags aren't distracting or redundant. Also, check that the characterization comes through in what is said, and that you have put in pauses that alter the pacing.

Now add in stage direction. Also add in a prop or two, like a drink, a phone or a toy. How can your characters' feelings and desires be shown in how they hold and treat the item in their hands? How can you have the characters move their bodies so that they communicate their desires this way rather than through their words?

# Where to next?

*The beginning of your story should describe an important moment in your narrative and compel the reader to keeping reading. The next chapter shows you how to go about creating successful opening lines and 'hooks' that will draw the reader into your story world.*

# 18

## Opening lines and hooks

The opening lines of your novel are the handshake, the look in the eye, the tone, the mood and the subtle yet powerful message that says to the reader, 'This is what to expect. This is worth the effort. This is a story worth reading.' Because of their importance, the opening lines need to be carefully sculpted.

The opening of your novel can be a work in progress alongside the work in progress. That is, feel free to compose your opening separately from the rest of the story. The insight, tone or narrative arc of the complete work may give you ideas on how to introduce the story, so it is worth considering saving the writing of the opening chapter for last. At that stage you will have a perspective on the story that could help you hit just the right note for the beginning.

*It is a truth universally acknowledged, that a single man in possession of a good fortune, must be in want of a wife.*
Jane Austen, *Pride and Prejudice*

*Many years later, as he faced the firing squad, Colonel Aureliano Buendía was to remember that distant afternoon when his father took him to discover ice.*
Gabriel García Márquez, *One Hundred Years of Solitude*

*I was born twice: first, as a baby girl, on a remarkably smogless Detroit day in January of 1960; and then again, as a teenage boy, in an emergency room near Petoskey, Michigan, in August of 1974.*
Jeffrey Eugenides, *Middlesex*

Why do some of the best opening lines in literature work so well?
- They set a tone for what is expected.
- They deliver the precise attitude of the narrator.
- They create an active scene.
- They ask a compelling question.
- They invite the readers into a wondrous world.
- They pique the reader's curiosity.
- They describe a pivotal moment that compels the reader to read more.

Opening lines that work less well include:
- a lengthy description of the setting
- inner dialogue of the main character and nothing else
- a static event, perhaps someone thinking or looking out the window
- a dream sequence
- a alarm going off, waking the main character to start his day.
- a fairy-tale beginning: 'Once upon a time …'
- a vivid description of the main character's appearance
- the backstory of the main character before he has a chance to do anything.

- directly addressing the reader: 'You're going to love this story; it's about …'
- action so perplexing and confusing that the reader has no idea what's going on
- dialogue that isn't immediately attributed to someone in the scene, leaving the reader to guess what's happening.

The opening lines have the potential to be the most powerful in the entire book. If your goal is to entice your readers, inviting them to join you on the journey, you will want to make your opening the best it can be.

## Write your opening scene

In ten minutes, write your opening scene as if it were a no-holds barred free write. Take as many ten-minute increments as you need to create a draft.

## Revise the scene

Use the following prompts to revise the scene as you are inspired.

1 What would it be like with a different point of view?
2 What would it be like from a different place in the action?
3 Create the scene in which raw emotion is revealed, then mention the general desires of the point-of-view character.
4 Does your scene have movement? What action can you put into the scene?
5 Consider the final scene from your notes. Is there a way to mention the final scene in your opening? For an example of this, see *To Kill a Mockingbird*.
6 Can you reflect the precise attitudes and emotions of your point-of-view character? For an example of this, see *Catcher in the Rye*.

## Analyse some opening lines

Study the first lines of great works of literature. This book is full of them, mostly in the chapter about the narrative voice. Or examine your own library or do an online search for 'great first lines from novels'. Note what these authors did that worked and what you liked about it. If you're ambitious, rewrite your opening paragraphs in the voice and tone of the great writers and note any insights you have.

## Where to next?

*In Part Four, we will see how to put all these elements of your story together as you embark on writing your first draft.*

# PART FOUR
Putting it all together

# 19

## Writing your first draft

Drafting is the first time you write the story; it is the nitty-gritty work of writing. You have a vision, a plot and characters, the characters have goals and desires, you have a narrative voice, you have notes on a three-act structure, you have a detailed setting, you've practised dialogue and opening lines. You know how to free write, how to find inspiration and how to set your timer. You have organization, files put away and a space in which to get your writing done. Nothing more can be done now except the actual writing.

Keep in mind, however, that this is only the first draft. This is not the time for literary greatness, nor the time for metaphorical gymnastics, nor the time for brilliance. It's time to get the story written.

Nicholas Sparks

*'Writing the last page of the first draft is the most enjoyable moment in writing. It's one of the most enjoyable moments in life, period.'*

The note-taking is over. The characterization is as complete as it needs to be. The story has been examined as thoroughly as possible without actually being a story. It's time to draft.

Drafting proves that you are a writer. Drafting means sitting down at your workspace (computer, big yellow tablet, Etch-A-Sketch, whatever) and putting word after word together, sentence after sentence until you get the story down on paper, all of it – beginning, middle and end.

Drafting means writing 'drunk'. When you write 'drunk' it means letting go of every inhibition and freely putting all your thoughts on paper. When people are drunk, they do stupid things, they talk to strangers, they dance on the table, yell and sing. They are the life of the party. They know no limits and they believe that the whole world loves them. You must draft with this kind of freedom.

Drafting requires the patience of gold miners as they dig through muddy water, hour after hour, discarding pounds of soil and muck, slowly going through each bit and hoping for a glimmer of gold. When they do, and the gold is pocketed, then they say it is worth all the dirty work. You must draft with this type of hope.

Drafting is much like what a sculptor does. He has put away the measurements, notes and sketches and finally picked up the hammer and chisel. He begins the actual sculpting: whacking and pounding. Bits of marble fly everywhere. Sculptors are committed to their vision and they're willing to make a mess to get to the general shape of their sculpture. They are not concerned with the look of the eyes or the smoothness of the skin; all they're after right now is general shape. You must draft with this kind of boldness.

This first draft is not for anyone's eyes but yours. It will be a hot mess. From it you will revise over and over, you will move things around, rewrite most of it, make a thousand changes and throw some of it out. But it is this draft that is the raw material of greatness. You can't take one step further in your novel unless you are committed to finishing the first draft.

## Judy Blume

*'People always wonder what kind of superhero power they'd like to have. I wanted the ability for someone to just open up my brain and take out the entire first draft and lay it down in front of me so I can just focus on the second, third and fourth drafts.'*

# How to write the first draft

1 Continue with your habits of working in small daily increments.

2 Keep your workspace and all your documents organized.

3 Review all your notes.

4 Don't worry about a brilliant beginning. (We'll address that in the revision stage.) Just tell the story. If you have to, start it with 'Once upon a time …'

5 Work chronologically, but allow yourself to skip around if you are inspired.

6 Keep this draft double-spaced so that, if you print, you've got room to make notes (and you *will* have notes).

7 Add page numbers for future reference. If for no other reason, your printer tray may break and all 200 pages fall on the floor. If that happens, you'll wish you had page numbers.

8 Write every day. Once momentum is lost, it is difficult to keep going. Even ten minutes will work. The habit of writing daily will keep you encouraged. Often, you'll find that when the timer dings, you have the will to go a little longer.

9 If you get stuck, simply ask yourself, 'What happens next?'

10 Do not rewrite at this stage. In fact, correct only the spelling and grammar that really bothers you. All corrections will come later. Use your notes. Go back to them as often as you need to. That's why they are there.

11 Focus on the story only. Details that slow you down (such as the colour of the assassin's eyes) are not worth the energy at this point.

12 Don't worry about chapter breaks, formatting or word count. Story is the ultimate goal.

13 Leave yourself notes if you need to.

14 Intimidated? Just break it down into small chunks. Draft a scene, a page, a paragraph at a time. You can write a novel in ten minutes a day.

15 Avoid going back to fix something; just make a note and keep moving forward. You can break this rule if you are especially inspired or find that the story is changing as you write it. This happens and, when it does, it means you're getting creative. Don't hinder this.

16 Write. Write. Write.

 Key idea

You *can* write a novel in ten minutes a day.

## WHAT TO AVOID

Beware of the following obstacles that might hinder your writing:

- **Arbitrary deadlines:** You don't need to put more pressure on yourself. This book will get written when it gets written.

- **Excuses not to write:** You'll always be tired. But you'll be glad you put in ten minutes. Those ten-minute segments add up quickly.

- **Talking too much about this to friends and family:** They may say thoughtless things, expect you to be J.K. Rowling, or demand an acknowledgement. You don't need additional pressure.

- **Concerns about publishing or marketing:** That will all come in time and your only objective right now is to write the book.

# What can wait until later drafts

You don't need to be concerned about any of the following until later:

## 1 Research

Cultural expectations, historical accuracies, styles, etc., which require an online search or a trip to the library, can wait. Make a note in the draft that you need to research something and return to it later. By doing this, you are keeping yourself focused. Research can take up huge amounts of time and you need your time to finish your first draft.

## 2 Chapter breaks

Don't worry about the exact organization of your story until you have the draft in your hands. You may see the logic to it later.

## 3 The killer opening and hook

Without question, your story's opening lines are important, but they need to be carefully sculpted, perhaps rewritten dozens of times. Put the opening aside and come back to it after the draft is written. You may have ideas on how the ending connects with the beginning (as *To Kill a Mockingbird* did) or you may see resonance throughout the book that can be introduced in the opening. Take your time with this. It is too important to be rushed.

## 4 Formatting

Draft in the way that makes you the most comfortable. Formatting, fonts, margins and line spacing should be addressed in the editing stage.

## 5 Literary devices

Symbols, themes and other things you learned about in high-school English can be sprinkled in during the revisions also.

## 6 Word count

Generally speaking, marketable novels run between 60–90,000 words. That doesn't mean that great novels haven't been longer or shorter, it just means that this range is the general market standard. During the revising and editing stage, word count for your desired market will be addressed, not before.

# Ten things to do if you are stuck

1  Just simply ask yourself, 'What happens next?'

2  Review your notes.

3  Do a free write on anything: the main character, the supporting characters, the setting, the plot or a specific prop you'll need.

4  Have a supporting character interrupt the life of the main character with a car accident, a sick child, a death in the family, an arrest, something that is surprising and stressful, and that could happen in real life.

5  Take a shower. The combination of heat, water and physical sensation often stimulates your brain and you may come out with an idea.

6  Take some exercise. This will also stimulate the brain.

7  Discuss the problem with one or two trusted friends.

8  Attack backstory. Write for ten minutes on your main character's childhood, a traumatic experience or most embarrassing moment.

9  Write for ten minutes on what everyone is wearing, and why. This may trigger you and you'll have a new idea.

10 Review all your notes, especially those from Chapter 4, *Write what you know*. You may find inspiration.

## Your finished draft

What you will have when you have finished is:

* a hot mess. More specifically, you'll have great starting point for the revisions and edits, which may take as long to complete as the first draft. Don't be discouraged by what needs to be done. This is all part of the process.

* nothing that needs to be seen by others, yet. Wait until things are less messy.

* something completely unpublishable. Don't even think of sending this to an agent or publisher.

When all the points have been made, all of the secrets have been revealed, the antagonist is punished and the protagonist's journey comes to a satisfying conclusion, when the all questions are answered and you can't think of anything else to add, you are then done with the first draft.

## Where to next?

*Put your first draft away for at least one month. When the month is over and you have a fresh, more objective opinion, you can begin the laborious task of revision. Now the real work begins.*

# 20

## Revising and editing

At the beginning of this book, you did an exercise to envision what your book was going to be. After months (maybe even years) of sculpting, you almost have this vision completed. The shape is right, the form is recognizable, you're satisfied with what's been written so far – it *is* complete, but it's far from finished.

The next part of the process is the revision and editing phase. This is the tedious and labour-intensive part of the writing process, but it is, arguably, the most significant. Only through the pathway of objective editing and revision will your manuscript arrive in the hands of your reader. Every good writer goes through the work of revisions and edits. Even this paragraph that you are reading was written and rewritten, arranged and edited, fretted over and changed in nearly every detail. This chapter breaks down the process into manageable chunks.

# Stephen King

*'How long you let your book rest – sort of like bread dough between kneadings – is entirely up to you, but I think it should be a minimum of six weeks.'*

# Making changes

When you revise you are making changes that have to do with logic, clarity and artistic choices. When you edit, you make changes that have to do with the technical mechanics of language: grammar, spelling and punctuation. Revision should come first, since great chunks of your story may have to be rewritten, such as the tense or the point-of-view character. When the content is artistically sound, the faster task of editing begins. Proofreading is an aspect of editing and deals with sentence errors, such as punctuation and spelling.

In this new stage, your purpose is no longer to create a story – adding sentences, chapters and plot points. Instead, it's time to take away, to omit and edit out, to rearrange and turn around, to reshape and rewrite. It's time to apply what is often credited to Hemingway but really said by novelist Peter De Vries and paraphrased here: 'You wrote drunk, it's time to edit sober.'

Don't make the mistake of thinking that you have no need to learn how to do this. To edit your own work, you need to create emotional distance between 'The End' and picking up the red pen. Putting your work in progress aside for few weeks may be all you need. You will need to make changes, perhaps painful ones, to make the book the best it can be. Most writers understand this and find a time of waiting helpful.

# Bridget McKenna, *The Little Book of Self-editing for Writers*

*'Good editing by the writer – before an outside editor ever sees your work – can make a difference between an okay book and a good one, or between a good book and a great one. It will also save you time and money.'*

You are not ready to revise and edit if:

- you think every word you put in your draft is precious
- you think your handle on the English language is flawless
- you trust only your computer's spellcheck function and no other proofreader
- you like the way your backstory goes on and on, can handle 'head-hopping' from one character to another and expect only your mother to buy copies
- the idea of cutting anything – any vague word, awkward sentence, self-indulgent paragraph, unnecessary chapter or useless character – appals you.

## Key idea

If you are not ready to revise and edit, then you are certainly not ready to publish.

If you are ready, then you'll be able to look at your manuscript objectively. You'll eliminate unnecessary characters with the brutality of a hitman. You'll change passive verbs to active ones with the precision of a surgeon. You won't be afraid to fill your literal or figurative recycling bin with dozens of pages. You'll be fearless and have a vision for completion.

Why go to all this trouble? It's because, in order to be read in an overly saturated market, your story must stand out. To have your name attached to something of inferior quality insults your hard work and the readers who read it. Stories are powerful and sloppy, careless writing weakens a story's power to move and shape the world. Errors also reflect on how you see yourself – if you don't care about being your best, no one else will take you seriously. In the revising and editing you will become better and stronger and you will see yourself improve in future books. For all these reasons, revising and editing are worth doing, even though the process can be discouraging and tedious.

# Revision step by step

In this section, the elements of your manuscript have been broken down into six steps. As you focus on each step, read through your manuscript repeatedly, focusing on each part at a time.

Doing the following exercises will be hard, exacting work. But if you look at this task as poring over a sculpture, square inch by square inch, looking for flaws and work on it in small, manageable chunks of time, perhaps even only ten minutes a day, then it is doable and not as intimidating. Each step in the revision process will take less work than the step before.

## NARRATIVE VOICE AND POINT OF VIEW

Any faults you find in the narrative voice or the point of view (POV) may require a huge rewrite. But if the novel needs to be rewritten, the story will be all the stronger for it. As you read through your manuscript, concentrate only on narrative voice and then ask yourself these questions, making notes or changes as you go. Don't move on to the next step until you are satisfied with this one.

1 Is your narrative voice a good fit for the genre? Not too morose for a comedy, and not too lighthearted for a drama? Accurate and believable for historical fiction? Not too archaic for a contemporary story?

2 Does your narrative voice enhance the plot?

3 Does your narrative voice work well with the setting? Do you feel they belong together and don't fight against each other?

4 If the point-of-view character is not the main character, is the relationship between the narrator and the biggest character a strong and believable one?

5 Do you feel that the reader knows too much? Not enough? Would switching from third person to first, or vice versa, make a difference for the better?

6 Are there any instances of the point of view switching to another person when it is not your intention?

7 Does your point-of-view character know something he shouldn't? Are there secrets that would be better hidden if the thoughts of the POV character were not known? Conversely,

is there insight to the mind of the POV character that would benefit the reader's experience?

8  Is the voice of the POV character an accurate portrayal of their education and characterization?

9  Is there the right amount of quirks and unique characteristics in their narration? Is there any inconsistency that needs to be corrected?

10  If you deliberately switch point of view in the story, is the distinction clear enough to the reader?

## Revising narrative voice and point of view

When you have finished answering all these questions, go back and make the necessary changes. Since these are major elements of the story, take all the time you need to correct them. Once done, continue on to the additional revising steps.

## CHARACTERS

Reread your manuscript, but this time look at the characters you have created. Ask yourself each of these questions and make notes.

1  Are your characters fully developed in every ABCD step (archetype, basic description, characterization and desires)?

2  Have you eliminated the possibility of cliché by adding detail in appropriate amounts?

3  Have you effectively shown, through your characters' actions and dialogue, what their inner desires are?

4  Are your descriptions of their physical appearance a boring laundry list or have you written them in a concise, creative way?

5  Does each character's dialogue have a style that is unique so that, theoretically, you would know who was speaking without any dialogue tag?

6  Are any characterizations you created for your characters, which are mentioned in the beginning, not needed in the end? For example, Scott is said to be a gun enthusiast, but guns, his

collection, his knowledge and his passion for guns play no role in the story. Can you omit this fact about him safely?

7 Are there any characters that come 'on stage' only once, and yet have been given too much description and background?

8 Are there any characters whose purpose in the story can be combined with other characters to make the story more concise?

9 Is there anything predictable or archetypical in your characters that you can revise to make them more unique and interesting?

10 Have you omitted all clunky references to past events, such as 'As you know, Bob, our team has lost eight straight games.'

## Revising characters

When you've finished making notes on all the above questions, return to your manuscript and make the necessary changes. Take your time: even if you do only a little work on this every day, you will eventually finish and your characters will be far more interesting and intriguing. Sculpt and resculpt your characters until you get them exactly right. Then move on to the next step.

## PLOT AND STORY STRUCTURE

Your purpose in working at the plot and story structure level is to make this story the leanest, clearest, most creative, most interesting story in your power. It is likely that your original vision has changed. That's great if it has – it means you've grown and tapped into fresh insight and new ideas. Reread your manuscript and go through the questions, making notes.

1 Does your story have an entertaining, unpredictable but logical story arc? Does it meet all the requirements for a good story? Is your ending conclusive, permanent and satisfactory?

2 Does your first act end no further in than at the quarter point?

3 Do the events in your second act progress in a logical manner, increasing in tension, putting your characters into more and more conflict?

4 Is the final decision that the main character makes feasible and engaging to the reader?

5  Is there a twist or an unexpected problem with this choice that makes the story even more interesting?

6  Does your third act tie up enough loose ends?

7  Have the characters sufficiently changed in the course of the story?

8  Are your scenes and sequences created and structured in an orderly fashion, increasing in tension?

9  Do you sense a push-and-pull feeling from the characters in every single scene, as they struggle with the pursuit of their goals?

10  Does the ending of each scene leave the reader with another question or a sense of urgency or a desire to find out what happens next?

11  Are there any extra characters that not needed in each scene?

12  Are there any scenes that seem dull and uninteresting? Can you omit them?

13  Do all your flashbacks come in logical places? Are they concise? Can you eliminate the flashback and reveal critical information in some other way?

## Revising plot and story structure

Return to your manuscript and make your changes, as you can, when you can. This could be potentially time-consuming but it is what craftsmanship is all about.

### WORLD BUILDING

In this section, you will be evaluating the development of your setting. Like the characters and the story, the setting needs to be as concise but as clear as possible. Review your manuscript and make notes.

1  Are all your descriptions consistent?

2  Are there any passages about history, geography or details of your world that can be omitted?

3   Are there any unanswered questions as to why this world is built the way it is, and are these unanswered questions critical to the story? Don't answer them if they're not.

4   Are the time, time frame, place, climate and culture explained enough to express the story in the most clear way?

## Revising world building

As before, use your notes on the questions to make the necessary changes. Even if you spend just ten minutes a day on this, your revisions will eventually be done and your book will be the better for it.

## DIALOGUE

Review each passage of dialogue and see whether you need to make any changes. Make notes on each question.

1   Do your dialogue tags reveal action or characterization but in a subtle way?

2   Will accents or dialects confuse the reader?

3   Are filler words like 'um' and 'er' omitted?

4   Are small-talk conversations omitted for the sake of pacing?

5   Are the sentences in the dialogue generally shorter than the sentences in the rest of the chapter?

6   Are there any long, unnecessary speeches that can be omitted?

7   Are there any actions or backstory or exposition that would be better revealed to the reader through dialogue?

8   Is your dialogue broken up into believable rhythms? Are there stops for bits of action?

9   Does your dialogue help reveal the conflicts of the characters?

10  Are there secrets in the characters' lives that can be hinted at but not fully revealed in the dialogue?

## Revising dialogue

Use your notes on dialogue to make your revisions. Take special note of the dialogue tags (*he said*, *she squawked*, *he yelled*). They should be subtle. They shouldn't draw attention to themselves. Use them to reveal action that occurs during the dialogue and to identify the speaker in case of confusion. They can also add emotional meaning, if it's done with a light touch. But if it doesn't do those things, take the tag out altogether.

# Editing step by step

The act of editing and proofreading is the literary equivalent of running the lint brush over your jacket, shining your shoes and brushing your teeth before the big dance. These little details work together to make a great first impression.

Lack of care in the areas of grammar, punctuation and word choice is a sure sign of an amateur. To be an excellent writer, one must be brutally disciplined in the basics of language. Anyone who thinks, 'Oh, my readers know what I meant', or 'The story is more important than grammar', or 'I'll let the publisher deal with it' is possibly delusional, setting themselves up for harsh reviews and likely to be disappointed. Take care to get this right.

As with revision, we are starting with the largest sections and moving into the smaller and trickier. In each of these four major issues – pacing, paragraphs, sentences and words – take the time to reread your manuscript and make notes on changes that you need to make. Don't be afraid to have several drafts of your manuscript. Most writers do this.

## PACING

Pacing is how fast or how slowly your story is progressing. A well-written novel speeds up and slows down throughout the story, taking the reader on an interesting, scenic and sometimes surprising ride.

During action scenes, make sentences shorter to increase the pace. During times of reflection, backstory and exposition, sentences and paragraphs can be longer, to slow things down so that the reader can keep track of the information. Skilled writers understand that pacing can be used to enhance conflict and increase tension.

## Editing for pacing

Reread your manuscript and notice the length of your sentences during the slower moments and compare them to the faster ones. If you see no difference, rewrite the sentences to make the journey more interesting.

## PARAGRAPHS

A novel should have paragraphs of varying lengths. This adds to the beauty of the story and contributes to the pacing. Your biggest pacing offenders may be lengthy passages of backstory, too much description, too much interior dialogue, and redundancies. Ask yourself these questions about your paragraphs, making notes as you go.

1 Are all the long paragraphs the shortest they can be?

2 Are there any instances of description that can be omitted?

3 Are there long paragraphs of backstory that bog down the pace?

4 Can the backstory be lightly distributed in other places?

5 Is there exposition or explanation that unnecessarily spoonfeeds the reader?

6 Do the paragraphs vary in length?

7 Do the paragraphs begin in different ways, so that one opens with dialogue, another with description, the next with action?

## Editing paragraphs

Review your manuscript again, but this time pay attention to the individual paragraphs. Use your notes to make your changes.

## SENTENCES

During the review of your paragraphs, it's likely that you trimmed a few sentences here and there. In case you skipped over a few, review the sentences in your manuscript and answer these questions about them, again making notes.

1 Are the sentences as tight and clear as they can possibly be?

2 Are the rules of good grammar followed?

3 Are all verb tenses consistent?

4 Do the sentences vary in length?

5 Are the sentences punctuated well? Are you confident in the placing of your commas?

6 Are the verbs precise and as clear as they can be?

7 Have you omitted excessive adjectives and adverbs?

8 Do the subjects and verbs agree?

9 Do you overuse pronouns so that there is confusion as to which noun they are replacing?

10 Are there any run-on sentences that need to be corrected?

11 Are there any incomplete sentences that need to be finished or omitted?

12 Are there any passive sentences that can be made more active? For example, 'The ball was thrown by me' is improved with a quick rewrite: 'I threw the ball.'

13 Are there any dangling participles? This means sentences that seem to have an awkward add-on that doesn't quite sound right. 'After graduating from obedience school, my sister was pleased with her puppy's progress' would be improved by switching it around: 'My sister was pleased with her puppy's progress after he graduated from obedience school.'

## Editing sentences

Review your manuscript again, but this time pay attention to the individual sentences. Use your notes to make your changes. If there are sentences that begin with 'It was' or 'There were', do a search and rewrite the sentence.

## WORDS

What is the best word? The best word is the one that is the clearest, often the shortest and, surprisingly, not the most aristocratic or 'writerly'. You are not a successful writer because you wrote a novel with lots of big words in it. You are successful because you wrote an engaging story was that was clear to your reader.

 Focus point

For more help, read a style guide such as Strunk and White's *Elements of Style*, call your old English teacher or research good writing resources on your own.

In your millionth reread of your manuscript, review your word choices. The fastest way to find unnecessary words is to use the search/find/replace feature on your word-processing application

1   Do a universal spellcheck. This is not your last line of defence, but your first. Check every word found through your search and confirm the changes.

2   Search for '-ly' words. These words are often adverbs and adverbs rarely add significance to the sentence. By searching for them by typing in 'ly', you will surely find many. The rule of thumb is to take it out first and then reread the sentence. If the meaning changes in a profound way, put it back in.

3   Search for 'be' verbs: *am, are, was, were, has, have, had*. Don't be discouraged if you find hundreds of instances of them. If they are used as a verb, replace them with something much stronger, more precise or more active. 'She had a pet cat named Charley who slept under her bed' would be better written as 'Charley, her pet cat, slept under the bed'.

4   Search for nouns that end in '-ation'. Often these words would be better written as verbs. For example, 'The losing team faced humiliation in the games' would be better written as 'The loss humiliated the team'.

5   Search for 'began to', 'started to', 'continued to', 'was able to'. These phrases serve no purpose. They weaken the verb they are sent to strengthen and should be omitted.

6  Search for 'some'. This is a weak adjective that means a vague amount. Rule of thumb: either substitute a specific amount or omit the idea altogether. 'Some's' evil twin is 'very' for the same reason, but it's not used as a quantity. Search for and omit it also.

7  Search for 'its/it's', 'their/there/they're', 'your/you're', 'loose/lose' and other common homophones. Spellcheck will miss these! Double-check that you are using the correct one for the sentence. Misuse can make you look like an amateur.

8  Search for 'then/than'. This is not quite a homophone problem – it could be a usage problem. If you're confused as to which to use, keep 'than' for comparisons and 'then' for everything else.

9  Search for ' apostrophes. Use apostrophes for two reasons: to show possession (Sidney's cat) and for contractions, which are two words put together, like *can't* or *don't*. Eliminate apostrophes from all other usage.

10 Search for 'should of', 'could of', 'would of'. This sounds right, but it isn't. Instead say, 'should have'. But even that, in comparison to other verbs, is weak. If you can, rewrite the sentence.

11 Search for two spaces after a full stop. Replace it with one space after a full stop. If you learned to type before the information age, then you were taught to do this for typesetting reasons. There is no reason to do this now and the error is strangely obvious. It's also an easy fix on the find/replace feature. This is not a word problem but a punctuation one.

## Editing for words

Once you have done the search/find/replace process for the most common problem words listed above, you should omit them, replace them or rewrite the sentence altogether. This is not an exhaustive list of problem words, but it is a start. Correct any other spelling mistakes you find, and then take the time to choose the best words: hunt out the weak, useless, redundant or misused.

The final step in the editing process is to read your manuscript aloud. Every word. This will definitely take a long time, but errors are revealed more quickly this way. Our mouths spot what our eyes have glossed over a million times.

## Where to next?

*The next step is to ask an experienced friend or a reading partner to read your novel for you. The following chapter explains what kinds of questions to ask your first readers – critique partners, critique groups or beta readers – as you prepare for publication.*

# 21

## Getting feedback

One of the most rewarding and satisfying parts of the writing process is the moment when you are ready to put your finished work into the hands of the first reader. Writers should get feedback from early readers about their novels before they publish or submit to agents. Thoughtful, precise and educated responses from readers can be a huge help in smoothing out the rough edges of a manuscript.

Writers can get their feedback either through a critique partner, critique groups or through beta readers. All of these methods are valuable and can benefit a writer during the revision and editing process.

Susanna Clark, *Jonathan Strange & Mr Norrell*

*"'Besides,' said Mr Norrell, "I really have no desire to write reviews of other people's books. Modern publications upon magic are the most pernicious things in the world, full of misinformation and wrong opinions."*

*"Then sir, you may say so. The ruder you are, the more the editors will be delighted."'*

# The critique partner

A critique partner is someone who gives feedback, usually with the understanding that this service will be reciprocated. The perfect critique partner is someone who can see your vision for your story, give honest feedback, and who perhaps does not write in your genre, so that there is no feeling of competition. A critique partner should have enough writing experience and knowledge to give specific and practical advice. A relationship between two critique partners must be a safe one, one that encourages each member in their writing goals, yet with the freedom to be honest.

A reliable critique partner is not easy to find. The perfect one for you may come out of relationships within a group of writers.

# Critique groups

Critique groups are small groups of writers who meet in person on a regular basis for the purpose of helping one another in their writing and publishing goals. Arguably, critique groups are the least effective way to get feedback, simply because everyone in the group wants attention and help. Individual opinions, particularly dissenting ones, are not free to be expressed. The quality of the advice is only as good as the quality of the writers. In a best-case scenario, all the members of the critique group are close in their skill level and experience and can encourage one another to aspire to be better. In the worst case, less experienced members can steer a writer in a wrong direction. Critique groups can, however, build much-needed community. Writing can be an isolating occupation and groups for writers can be a great source of practical tips and inspiration.

The best critique groups:

- meet regularly with clearly explained expectations
- make a deliberate effort to have everyone's manuscript read and evaluated
- welcome differences of opinion and work to see things from others' points of view
- are encouraging, safe places for new and emerging writers
- have a spirit of fun in them, not one of competition
- celebrate publishing successes of all kinds
- include writers of all skill levels and gently encourage everyone.

# Beta readers

Beta readers are any first readers who are qualified to make editorial observations. They often read voluntarily without any expectation of the favour being returned. The term 'beta reader' is gently stolen from computer software technology. In the 'beta' phase, a new program or app is tried out by an objective party and examined for bugs or quirks. That's exactly what a beta reader can do for your manuscript: find the bugs and quirks and point out ways to improve.

The best beta readers:

- read the kinds of books you have written. If you write romance, you would want a reader who had read dozens of romances. A good friend who only reads fantasy might not have the insight that a romance reader would have
- can be free to be honest with you. You should be able to receive an unpleasant response from them without taking it personally
- commit to not just a read-through but to critical thinking, answering questions, and perhaps even a phone call or an email
- have good communication skills, are avid readers, know good books and think critically
- work quickly and won't take weeks or months to return your manuscript to you
- will support your writing dreams
- are not your spouse or your parents. Family members are often a little too close to you to give an objective opinion.

# How to find a reader

There are many different ways to meet other writers. Either in real life or online, writing groups are almost everywhere. Check Google groups, Facebook, GoodReads, local writing groups that might be found on MeetUp.com, your local library, and English teachers in your local schools. Twitter has several hashtags for writers: #amwriting, #storydam, #K8chat, #write, #wip and #10MinNovelists. 10 Minute Novelists is the Facebook group created by the author of this book in 2014 to find other time-crunched writers. From this group, many writers have found readers and helpful suggestions for their work in progress. Within the group, many writers have found a formal critique group, beta readers or a knowledgeable critique partner.

## QUESTIONS TO ASK YOUR READER

It is far more effective for your reader to know what to look for in the book. If you can't provide specific questions for them to answer, the only response you may get is a 'Yeah, I liked it.' Create specific questions for them to answer, or use the questions provided below.

1 What did you like most about the book?

2 What did you like least?

3 Who was your favourite character, and why?

4 Was there anything that was too unbelievable or implausible?

5 At the same time, was anything predictable?

6 Were there any places you skipped over? If so, why?

7 Did you feel that the story moved at a comfortable pace? Or was it too slow or too fast?

8 Did you fully understand the objectives of the characters? Were their obstacles interesting and plausible?

9 Were there any unanswered questions or plot holes?

10 Did you find the themes to be too preachy?

11 What was your favourite part?

12 Were the descriptions clear?

13 Do you have any suggestions for how I could improve this book?

14 Would you recommend this book to a friend?

# WHAT TO DO WITH FEEDBACK

Receiving feedback from thoughtful readers is rewarding, but it is risky too. By allowing readers to enjoy your completed draft, you run the risk of criticism or being misunderstood or disrespected. But it is far easier to get helpful advice from experienced people who are close to you than a rejection email from a publisher. If you are going to take your writing seriously, then you'll also need to be open to criticism and suggestions. Fiction writing is not a career path for the thin-skinned.

Here are some tips for what to do with the feedback you receive:

1  **Don't take negativity personally.** While it is difficult to pour your heart and soul into your first novel without being protective of it, take all suggestions as lightly as possible. If you couldn't handle honest feedback, you shouldn't have asked for it.

2  **Weigh each suggestion carefully.** Some will be obvious, such as spelling or punctuation errors. But others, like character, plot or structure suggestions, might require rewrites. Fix the easy things first and then line up your story's vision with the suggestion. If it's valid, make the change. You can always change it back. Remember, you are still the sculptor. Your opinion, at this point, is the only one that really counts.

3  **Keep the glowing reports.** File away all of the 'This was awesome!' notes. You'll need them in the future when others aren't so generous.

4  **Don't defend yourself.** If you feel misunderstood, keep your emotions under control, rethink any suggestions and move on.

5  **Keep in mind that some readers just won't get you.** If you have five respected beta readers and all but one rave about how good it is, remember that this is a plausible average for every bestseller out there. This is the beauty of art. A particular book will not please everyone.

6  **Be grateful.** Regardless of whether or not you agree with your readers' comments, thank them for their feedback. You may need them again in the future.

7  **Be careful.** The more readers who view your finished manuscript, the more differing opinions you may receive. Too few readers and you may not have an objective report on the quality of your work. Too many, and the many different suggestions can be confusing.

# Contact writers' groups and readers

1 Do a search on Google, Facebook, Meetup, GoodReads or Twitter for writers, writing groups or critique groups. Contact them or join them and find out what services they have for groups.

2 Ask your local library. Often librarians work closely with authors of all kinds. They may know of a group of writers or they may want to create one. You can create your own through meetup. com or Craigslist or through local adult education classes.

3 List all the people in your life who have editorial experience or who are avid readers. Contact them and ask them if they would read your work. Send them your manuscript through email as an attachment or set up a Google document so they can write on it. Have your questions ready.

## Where to next?

*The next chapter tells you how to go about publishing your novel. It describes the pros and cons of the various publishing options, from self-publishing to finding a traditional publisher. It explains what literary agents do, where you can meet them and how to approach them.*

# 22

## Finding a publisher

In the light of the fact that world literacy is at an all-time high and the new digital formats mean that publishing books and finding readers has never been simpler, you would think things would be easy for an emerging author. Yet, because of the massive amounts of books being published in all formats, by authors with all types of experience, the competition for readers and publishers has never been tougher.

There are several ways that you can publish but, before you make a choice, you need to inform yourself about various options, what you can expect with them and how they best fit the needs of your book. This chapter explains the various options and the pros and cons of each.

Edna St Vincent Millay

*'A person who publishes a book wilfully appears before the populace with his pants down. If it is a good book nothing can hurt him. If it is a bad book nothing can help him.'*

There has never been an easier time, as Edna St Vincent Millay said, for an author to 'appear before the populace with his pants down'. You could, theoretically, publish your own work, either in print or in digital formats, in a matter of hours. If this is the first novel you have written then, sadly, it is unlikely to be a *New York Times* bestseller. It is, however, a stepping-stone for future books.

Without exception, no best, selling author achieved their fame and fortune overnight. All spent years writing many unpublished or unreadable novels, perfecting their craft, trying new things, learning, reading and writing until opportunities opened for them. However, that doesn't mean that you can't publish at all. Self-publishing could be a feasible option for you.

# Self-publishing

Self-publishing means that you, and only you, are taking responsibility for every aspect of the publication of your book. This includes the title, the cover art, the formatting, the printing, the distributing and the marketing. Self-publishing allows you to have all the control of every aspect of your publication process, but it may require you either to do things you haven't done before or to hire someone to do them for you.

Before you decide to self-publish, ask yourself these questions:

1 Do you want to gain readers outside your friends and family?
2 Do you want the responsibility of designing, publishing and marketing?
3 Are you willing to invest time and energy in a marketing plan?
4 Are you willing to take chances? Are you willing to be a public speaker? Grow a social media presence? Promote yourself as an author?

If you answer no to any of these questions, your book may not be a good choice for self-publishing. But if you say yes, then you have another adventure ahead of you – one that can open doors for your writing, allow you to meet people from all over the world, and stretch your skills.

Self-publishing, either in paperback or digital formats, is the act of publishing as your own independent entity. It is, from a business perspective, creating a new product and offering it to the world. Self-publishing allows writers to have immense freedom but it also puts immense responsibility on their shoulders.

In order to have a professional-looking book, self-publishers must be responsible for organizing the following aspects of publication.

## FORMATTING

Many self-publishing authors teach themselves how to do this. Smashwords offers a free .pdf to explain how to do this for their authors. Or you can hire someone to do it for you. Online publishing houses like Kindle Direct require special formats. You will need to learn how to manage them, either by researching all you can or by trial and error. Consider getting advice from other experienced self-published writers. The writing groups listed at the end of this book will most likely have writers who may be able to advise you.

## COVER ART DESIGN

The cover art is not a place to do it yourself, unless you are a professional graphic designer or illustrator. Since the cover is the first thing the reader sees, it is critical that yours doesn't look like a clip-art creation. Consider hiring a freelance artist to design a cover worthy of your book and its readers.

## EDITING AND PROOFREADING

Many self-published authors are often so enthusiastic to get their work out into the marketplace that they overlook the value of a good editor or proofreader. Even if you followed all the steps in the chapter about editing, ask a pro to give a once-over too.

## ISBN

To be sold in general retail markets, your book will need an ISBN (International Standard Book Number). The 13-digit code makes it possible to track and identify your book. Many online self-publishing sites such as Kindle Direct provide one for you and you'll need one for each format in which you publish. If you choose another service, you may have to pay for your ISBN.

## PRINTING

If you want your book to be printed as a paperback rather than digitally, you will need to choose a service to be your printer. Each of these may have start-up costs, printing costs and cover design expenses. Or you may want to go with a print-on-demand service, which is more economical. Createspace is an example of a print-on-demand service and many hundreds of self-published authors have used it.

 Key idea

Many online self-publishing services have easy, step-by-step instructions so that complete beginners can have their novels ready for sale in a matter of days. The convenience and ease of self-publishing makes it a tempting choice for many writers.

# Traditional publishing

Traditional publishing is generally what everyone thinks of when they think of publishing. The major publishers include Penguin Random House, Macmillan, Simon & Schuster, HarperCollins and Hachette and their subdivisions. These publishing houses have the means to put their titles in local bookstores, buy ad space on GoodReads and be the people behind the bestsellers. Traditional publishers are often a part of a vast corporation with huge staffs that report to executives. These traditional publishers can offer their authors great exposure and have the best chance of getting their author's books into bookstore chains. But the publishers will make *all* the decisions regarding design. The author who signs with a traditional publisher may get more opportunities for sales than with other routes, but gives up more control and more of their rights.

You might prefer the idea of being published by a smaller, independent publisher rather than one of the major publishing houses. Independents are usually small publishing houses producing books to fit their specific criteria. Otherwise the main difference between independent publishers and traditional publishers is usually in the resources they have available. Independents tend to have fewer authors and fewer titles than traditional publishers. They also often have smaller staffs and smaller budgets. This means that, while they may not be able to do what bigger publishers can do, they can give their authors more personal attention, take chances on unknown authors and put their books in untraditional places. Like traditional publishers, they usually make the decisions regarding format, cover and design and they also handle all the decisions such as copyright.

## Focus point

Before submitting to an indie house, be thorough in your research and find out what they are looking for and what they require.

# Literary agents

While some independent publishing houses will work directly with authors and not with agents, the major publishing houses almost always require a new author to be represented by an agent. Often they have long relationships with specific agents and trust their wisdom. If you want to go with one of the main traditional publishing houses, it is more than likely that you will need to get an agent first.

The role of the literary agent is to represent an author's work and pitch it to appropriate publishing houses. If the publisher likes it and wants to move forward with a contract, it is the literary agent who communicates to the publisher the desires of the author and negotiates the deal. Since the rise of self- and independent publishing, the roles of the literary agent have changed. In addition to working closely with publishers in the way they always have, many agents are now also 'coaches' who will direct an author on ways to improve their work. The relationship between an author and an agent is not employee/employer but more like a business relationship or a team. The team's goal is to agree what success looks like for the author, and then do everything they can to make the author successful.

## HOW TO FIND AN AGENT

Finding the right literary agent is lot like finding a good spouse. You need to know what you're looking for, you need to make the best impression possible, and you need to be patient – starting the relationship slowly and getting to know each other, until you're sure you have the right fit.

Research the genres that agents represent. Check out the websites of as many agents as you can and find out whether they represent your genre. Do not contact them if they only represent children's books and poetry and you have a great sci-fi thriller. Instead, narrow your selection of agents to those who are looking for your type of book.

Check out their authors. You can learn much about an agent from the authors he represents. What publishing houses are most often represented? How many books do these authors have published? You could even contact the author and ask them if they are happy with their agent. But do *not* ask them to help you meet the agent or pitch your book for you. This is inappropriate. The relationship between an author and an agent, if it is a good one, is one full of trust – they are business partners – so don't ask an author to do anything that might breach that trust.

Find out the best way to approach the agent. Most agents state their submissions policy on their website. Respect it. If it says 'Not accepting unsolicited submissions', it means that any submission you send will be ignored. If it says 'Send queries via email only', don't assume that a posted letter will stand out. It will just be annoying and leave a bad first impression. If the agent communicates that a query letter is the best way to introduce yourself, then take the time to write the best query letter you can.

If you're looking for an agent, choose one that:

- has a clear and informative website, blog or other social media presence
- keeps up with changes in publishing
- has many good relationships with all kinds of publishers. This is indicated by the different houses for which this agent's authors have written. The agent's website should provide you with this information.
- is willing to be flexible with their ever-changing roles. An agent may use a blog or newsletter to communicate to current and potential authors about changes and trends in publishing.
- is easily accessible. This means that agents are willing to meet new writers at conferences, answer questions on their blog or speak at events. Then, once they sign an author, they should be easy to communicate with through phone or email.
- works on commission. Any agent that insists on being paid in advance for 'reading' or any other service is unscrupulous and should be avoided, especially by new writers who just want to get their name out there.

## Focus point

Before signing with any agent, do thorough research on their past clients. Study the published works of these clients. Find out what publishing houses they've worked for in the past and discover what others have said about them.

## QUERY LETTERS

Query letters are introductory letters, sent either by post or by email, which offer an agent the general idea of a book. Query letters are short, succinct, full of only necessary information, and should always be as professional as possible. A query letter gives agents a chance to meet you in a matter of seconds – and often they know, within the first few lines, whether they are interested in you or not.

A first line of the query letter should include the basic facts about your story, the genre, the word count, and one sentence that describes what it is about: 'My 75,000-word historical romance is about a Union soldier and an orphaned Southern belle who were separated during the burning of Atlanta and then were reunited 15 years later.'

The next part of the query letter is the summary of the story. It states the name of the main character and tells the story in six to ten sentences. Include only the most important characters, the setting and the main plot. Make sure the verbs you use are the strongest possible and your descriptors of your characters are vibrant and clear. The last sentence of this summary should describe (in the form of a question) the choice your main character has to make – the one with the two mutually exclusive desires – and it is *this* that is the most important sentence in the entire letter. 'Will Emmeline choose to return to Wade's arms or marry Beauford, the man who restored her fortune after the war?'

The next part of the query describes your writing experience. If you have any professional writing credentials, list them here. This would include any previous publications (fiction and non-fiction), blogging and education in the writing field. Keep this to four to six sentences. If you don't have any experience, don't apologize for it, just skip this part.

The next part of the query should be whatever the agents require. Sometimes they want sample pages pasted into the email, sometimes they want attachments. If you do not follow their instructions carefully, you run the risk of being ignored.

Close your query graciously and professionally: 'Thank you for your consideration.'

## The most common mistakes in queries

People can easily make serious mistakes in their query letter with realizing it. Here are some of the most common:

- **Writing an overly cute, shocking or cheesy beginning to your query**
  Most agents would prefer you get to the point.
- **Overwriting the summary**
  Keep this as short as you can make it. Your book may have a hundred characters, you may have many subplots and you may have dozens of settings, but in *this* summary, keep it as simple as you can.
- **Overformatting the query**
  A query is a lot like a CV or résumé. It should look as professional as possible. Omit emoticons, coloured type, all caps or unusual fonts.

- **Overstating your accomplishment**
  Writing a novel is a big deal and few people have done it, but agents receive thousands of query letters a year from people who have written a novel and want representation. If you claim yours is 'the next bestseller' or 'just like Harry Potter' or 'better than James Patterson', you'll be seen as delusional and not taken seriously. Keep these thoughts to yourself.

- **Quoting what others have said about your novel**
  Agents don't care what your friend says (unless your friend is a literary great, and then only sometimes). This also smacks of unprofessionalism (perhaps even delusion) and is best left out of a query.

- **What actor should play your characters in the film, or *how this would make a great movie!***
  If authors are honest, they've already thought about this. They may have even 'hired' their dream director and written the movie score. While this is fun to think about, it will not impress an agent. Most literary agents don't even deal with film rights, so comments like this are nonsensical and not worth mentioning.

- **Your cover art ideas**
  Perhaps later, well after your representation contract is signed and you've had several conversations with your agent about the plan for this book, you can bring up your cover ideas – but only if your publisher gives you that freedom, and they probably won't.

- **Demands for payment**
  Even if mentioning this wasn't completely arrogant, an agent is not the person who writes the cheques; the publisher is. Stay humble and let the agent be the one to bring up money.

- **Your childhood fantasies**
  Don't mention that you've been writing since you were five. *Every* writer can say that. It's more important to say what you are doing with your desires now than what you did with them then.

## How long should you wait for a reply?

Most agents respond to query letters within four weeks. However,
it isn't always possible for an agent to personally respond to every
query letter sent to them. If you do not hear from an agent after a
month, it's likely that they aren't interested. Move on to the next
agent and try again. As tempting as it may be to send a follow-
up email, or to call or contact the agent to ask why they have not
responded, resist this temptation. Agents know what they want
and they have no obligation to explain themselves. For the sake of
professionalism, take the high road, vent privately, and keep going.

# Conferences

A great way to meet agents is by going to a conference. Research
conferences for your genre and attend them, preparing yourself for
a chance to pitch your book idea to an agent. A good pitch could
result in future emails; an agent could request sample pages and
possibly give you feedback on how to improve. Many agents prefer
meeting authors this way. It gives them a chance to look authors in
the eye, shake their hand and get a feel for how they could work
together in this business relationship.

If an agent requests a *partial*, this means that they want to see the
first few samples pages of your novel. This could mean 10–50 pages.
If they do, follow their instructions to the letter. Make sure that your
submitted partial is as neat and professional as it can be.

If they don't ask for a partial, then they may ask for a synopsis. A
synopsis is a description of the book of between four and ten pages.
Usually written in the present tense, this gives the agent or publisher

a complete summary of the whole story. The synopsis can leave out much of the detail, but should include all major characters, all major plot points and a clear ending. Unlike the query letter, the synopsis includes more detail of the other characters and setting and reveals the final choice that the main character made.

## Focus point

Because the market is so saturated, publishers are highly selective. It is tempting to believe that, because it is written, your first book will automatically find an agent or publisher immediately. While it's not impossible, it is pretty improbable. You wouldn't expect a new watercolour artist to get into the Louvre with their first painting or a three-year piano student to play at Carnegie Hall. The same is true in the publishing industry.

## Key idea

Publishers, editors and agents are looking for masters of the craft who conduct themselves professionally, not newbies who aren't willing to learn and grow.

# How to turn the odds in your favour

Write the best book you can write. Get as much advice as possible. Write and rewrite and rewrite. Read all the writing books you can get your hands on. Be humble and teachable.

Then write another book. The process will improve your skills. You can easily start a new story-sculpting experience by using the exercises from this book from the plot chapter to the drafting chapter. The second book will most likely be easier to write.

Most traditionally published authors have several unpublished books in their files that will never see a reader. It was through these books that these authors learned their craft. This can be a slow and discouraging process but *good art takes time*. And, as you've learned, you can accomplish great things in just a few minutes a day.

Work hard, be humble and learn all you can, and you *will* get better over time. And you *will* get the attention of industry professionals.

Don't forget to celebrate your accomplishment. This completion of your ten-minute novel is worthy of at the very least, a pat on the back. Break out the champagne if you can.

Congratulations! You are a novelist!

 ## Philip Pullman

*'After nourishment, shelter and companionship, stories are the thing we need most in the world.'*

# References

Below is a list of references and other writing resources that can help you hone your craft and encourage you in your writing journey. Titles are arranged according to the corresponding parts of the book.

## PART ONE: ARRANGING YOUR WRITING AROUND YOUR LIFE

### Envisioning and planning

Cameron, Julia, *The Artist's Way* (Tarcher, 1992)

Elsheimer, Janice, *The Creative Call* (Shaw Books, 2001)

Pressfield, Steven, *Do the Work* (The Domino Project, 2011)

Upland, Brenda, *If You Want to Write: A Book about Art, Independence and Spirit* (Greywolf Press, 1983)

### Organizing your time and creating your space

Cilley, Marla, *Sink Reflections* (Bantam, 2002)

Currey, Mason, *Daily Rituals: How Artists Work* (Knopf, 2013)

Emmett, Rita, *The Procrastinator's Handbook: Mastering the Art of Doing It Now* (Walker & Company, 2000)

Morgenstern, Julie, *When Organizing Isn't Enough: Shed Your Stuff, Change Your Life* (Fireside Books, 2008)

Young, Pam, *Sidetracked Home Executives(TM): From Pigpen to Paradise* (Grand Central Publishing, 2001)

## PART TWO: THINKING LIKE A WRITER

Carson, Shelley H., *The Creative Brain* (Jossey-Bass, 2010)

Clark, Roy Peter, *Writing Tools: 50 Essential Strategies for Every Writer* (Little Brown and Company, 2006)

Dillard, Annie, *The Writing Life* (Harper Perennial, 1989)

Edgerton, Les, *Finding Your Voice: How to Put Personality in Your Writing* (Writer's Digest Books, 2003)

Goldberg, Natalie, *Writing Down the Bones: Freeing the Writer Within* (Shambhala, 1986)

Johnson, Steven, *Where Good Ideas Come From: The Natural History of Innovation* (Riverhead Hardcover, 2010)

Maass, Donald, *Writing 21st-century Fiction: High-Impact Techniques for Exceptional Storytelling* (Writer's Digest Books, 2012)

McKee, Robert, *Story: Substance, Structure, Style and the Principles of Screenwriting* (It Books, 1997)

Michalko, Michael, *Thinkertoys: A Handbook of Creative-Thinking Techniques* (Ten Speed Press, 1991)

Mixon, Victoria, *The Art & Craft of Fiction: A Practitioner's Manual* (La Favorita Press, 2010)

Mixon, Victoria, *The Art & Craft of Story: 2nd Practitioner's Manual* (La Favorita Press, 2010)

Pressfield, Steven, *The War of Art: Break through the Blocks & Win Your Inner Creative Battles* (Warner Books, 2002)

Rifer Johnston, Marcia, *Word Up! How to Write Powerful Sentences and Paragraphs* (Northwest Brainstorms Publishing, 2013)

Sawyer, R. Keith, *Explaining Creativity: The Science of Innovation* (Oxford University Press, 2006)

Schubert, Edmund R., *How to Write Magical Words: A Writer's Companion* (Bella Rosa Books, 2011)

Yolen, Jane, *Take Joy: A Writer's Guide to Loving the Craft* (Writer's Digest Books, 2003)

## PART THREE: SCULPTING THE ELEMENTS OF STORY

### Story, plot and structure

Alderson, Martha, *The Plot Whisperer: Secrets of Story Structure Any Writer Can Master* (Adams Media, 2011)

Booker, Christopher, *The Seven Basic Plots* (Bloomsbury Academic, 2004)

Campbell, Joseph, *The Hero with a Thousand Faces* (Princeton University Press, 1949)

Gerke, Jeff, *Plot Versus Character: A Balanced Approach to Writing Great Fiction* (Writer's Digest Books, 2010)

Ingermanson, Randy, *Writing Fiction for Dummies* (Wiley Publishing, Inc., 2009)

Scott Bell, James, *Plot and Structure* (Writer's Digest Books, 2004)

Weiland, K.M., *Outlining Your Novel: Map Your Way to Success* (PenForASword Publishing, 2011)

### Genre and world building

Alleyn, Susanne, *Medieval Underpants and Other Blunders: A Writer's (and Editor's) Guide to Keeping Historical Fiction Free of Common Anachronisms, Errors, and Myths* (Spyderwort Press, 2012)

Athans, Philip, *The Guide to Writing Fantasy and Science Fiction: 6 Steps to Writing and Publishing Your Bestseller!* (Adams Media Corporation, 2010)

Brooks, Terry, *The Writer's Complete Fantasy Reference: An Indispensable Compendium of Myth and Magic* (Walking Stick Press, 1998)

Grant, Vanessa, *Writing Romance* (Self Counsel Press, 1997)

Highsmith, Patricia, *Plotting and Writing Suspense Fiction* (St. Martin's Griffin, 1990)

James, P.D., *Talking about Detective Fiction* (Knopf, 2009)

Scott Card, Orson, *How to Write Science Fiction & Fantasy* (Writer's Digest Books, 2001)

### The characters

Ackerman, Angela, *The Emotion Thesaurus: A Writer's Guide to Character Expression* (JADD Publishing, 2012)

Brooks, Larry, *Story Engineering: Character Development, Story Concept, Scene Construction* (F&W, 2011)

Cowden, Tami D., *Complete Writer's Guide to Heroes and Heroines: Sixteen Master Archetypes* (Lone Eagle, 2000)

Kress, Nancy, *Characters, Emotion & Viewpoint: Techniques and Exercises for Crafting Dynamic Characters and Effective Viewpoints* (Writer's Digest Books, 2005)

Scott Card, Orson, *Characters & Viewpoint* (Writer's Digest, 1998)

# PART FOUR: PUTTING IT ALL TOGETHER

**Drafting and general writing**

King, Stephen, *On Writing* (Pocket Books, 1999)

Lamott, Anne, *Bird by Bird* (Anchor, 1994)

Lerner, Betsy, *The Forest for the Trees* (Riverhead Trade, 2000)

Lukeman, Noah, *The First Five Pages* (Touchstone, 2000)

Maass, Donald, *Writing the Breakout Novel* (Writer's Digest, 2001)

Mittelmark, Howard, *How Not to Write a Novel: 200 Classic Mistakes and How to Avoid Them – A Misstep-by-Misstep Guide* (William Morrow Paperbacks, 2008)

Orwell, George, *Why I Write* (Penguin Books, 1946)

Stein, Sol, *Stein on Writing: A Master Editor of Some of the Most Successful Writers of Our Century Shares His Craft Techniques and Strategies* (St. Martin's Griffin, 1995)

Stein, Sol, *How to Grow a Novel: The Most Common Mistakes Writers Make and How to Overcome Them* (St. Martin's Griffin, 1999)

**Revising and editing**

Browne, Renni, *Self-editing for Fiction Writers: How to Edit Yourself into Print* (William Morrow Paperbacks, 2004)

Lane, Barry, *The Reviser's Toolbox* (Discover Writing Press, 1998)

McKenna, Bridget, *The Little Book of Self-editing* (Ravenscourt Press, 2014)

Strunk, William and White, E.B., *The Elements of Style*, 4th edn (Longman, 1999)

Truss, Lynne, *Eats, Shoots & Leaves: The Zero Tolerance Approach to Punctuation* (Penguin, 2003)

Yardley, Cathy, *Rock Your Revisions: A Simple System for Revising Your Novel* (Rock Your Writing, 2012)

# Novelists' associations, guilds and organizations

## UNITED STATES

African American Online Writers Guild
http://www.blackwriters.org/

Alliance of Independent Authors
http://allianceindependentauthors.org/

American Christian Fiction Writers http://www.acfw.com/

American Christian Writers Association
http://regaforder.wordpress.com/

American Crime Writers League http://www.acwl.org/

Association of Writers and Writing Programs
https://www.awpwriter.org/

Authors Guild http://www.authorsguild.org/

Cat Writers' Association http://catwriters.com/wp_meow/

Dog Writers of America http://www.dwaa.org/

Erotica Readers and Writers Association
http://www.erotica-readers.com/

Heartland Writers Guild http://heartlandwriters.org/

Horror Writers Association http://horror.org/

International Association of Aspiring Authors
http://www.associationofaspiringauthors.com/

International Association of Crime Writers http://www.iacw.org/

International Science Writers Association
http://www.internationalsciencewriters.org/

International Women's Writing Guild http://www.iwwg.org/

Midwest Writers http://www.midwestwriters.org/

Military Writers Society of America http://www.mwsadispatches.com/

Mystery Writers of America http://mysterywriters.org/

National Association of Independent Writers and Editors
http://naiwe.com/

National League of American Pen Women http://www.nlapw.org/

Northwest Christian Writers Association
http://www.nwchristianwriters.org/

Novelists Inc http://www.ninc.com/

Ozark Creative Writers http://ozarkcreativewriters.com/

Pacific Northwest Writers Association http://www.pnwa.org/

PEN American Center https://www.pen.org/

Rocky Mountain Fiction Writers http://rmfw.org/

Romance Writers of America http://www.rwa.org/

Science Fiction and Fantasy Writers Association http://www.sfwa.org/

Sisters in Crime http://www.sistersincrime.org/

Society of Southwestern Authors http://www.ssa-az.org/

Southeastern Writers Association http://southeasternwriters.org/

Western Writers of America http://westernwriters.org/

Women Writing the West http://www.womenwritingthewest.org/

## UNITED KINGDOM

Alliance of Indpendent Authors http://allianceindependentauthors.org/

Association of Christian Writers http://www.christianwriters.org.uk/

British Fantasy Society http://www.britishfantasysociety.org/

British Science Fiction Association http://www.bsfa.co.uk/

Crime Writer's Association http://thecwa.co.uk/

Historical Novel Society http://historicalnovelsociety.org/

Historical Writers' Association http://www.thehwa.co.uk/

National Association of Writers' Groups http://www.nawg.co.uk/

Romantic Novelists Association http://www.rna-uk.org/

Science Fiction Research Association http://www.sfra.org/

Society of Authors http://www.societyofauthors.org/

## AUSTRALIA & NEW ZEALAND

Australian Crime Writers Association http://www.austcrimewriters.com/

Australian Society of Authors www.asauthors.org

Australian Horror Writers Association http://www.australianhorror.com/

Fellowship of Australian Authors http://www.writers.asn.au/

New Zealand Society of Authors http://www.authors.org.nz/

Romance Writers of Australia http://www.romanceaustralia.com/

Romance Writers of New Zealand http://www.romancewriters.co.nz/about/

Science Fiction and Fantasy Association of New Zealand http://www.sffanz.org.nz/

## CANADA

Alberta Romance Writers Association http://albertaromancewriters.com/

Canada Authors http://canadianauthors.org/

Canada's National Association of Speculative Fiction Professionals http://northbynotwest.com/sfcanada-wp/

Canadian Society of Children's Authors, Illustrators and Performers http://www.canscaip.org/

Crime Writers of Canada http://www.crimewriterscanada.com/

Professional Writers Association of Canada http://www.crimewriterscanada.com/

Writers Guild of Canada http://www.writersguildofcanada.com/

The Word Guild https://thewordguild.com

## INTERNATIONAL

International Association of Aspiring Writers http://www.associationofaspiringauthors.com/

International Association of Crime Writers http://www.iacw.org/

International Science Writers Association http://www.internationalsciencewriters.org/

International Women's Writing Guild http://www.iwwg.org/

# Index